BEYOND WINNING

The Timeless Wisdom of Great Philosopher Coaches

Gary M. Walton, PhD
President, Foundation for Teaching Economics
Professor of Management and Economics
University of California, Davis

Leisure Press
Champaign, IL

Library of Congress Cataloging-in-Publication Data

Walton, Gary M.
   Beyond Winning : the timeless wisdom of great philosopher coaches
/ Gary M. Walton.
     p.   cm.
   Includes bibliographical references.
   ISBN 0-88011-453-3
   1. Coaches (Athletics)--United States--Biography.   2. Coaching
(Athletics)--Philosophy.   I. Title.
GV697.A1W35   1992
796'.077'0922--dc20
[B]   91-23761
                                          CIP

ISBN: 0-88011-453-3

Acquisitions Editor: Brian Holding
Developmental Editor: John Robert King
Managing Editor: Kari Nelson
Assistant Editor: Elizabeth Bridgett
Copyeditor: Vickie West
Proofreader: Kathy Bennett
Production Director: Ernie Noa
Typesetter: Sandra Meier
Text Design: Keith Blomberg
Text Layout: Sandra Meier
Cover Design: Tim Offenstein
Printer: Versa Press

Leisure Press books are available at special discounts for bulk purchase for sales promotions, premiums, fund-raising, or educational use. Special editions or book excerpts can also be created to specification. For details, contact the Special Sales Manager at Leisure Press.

Printed in the United States of America   10 9 8 7 6 5 4 3

Leisure Press
A Division of Human Kinetics
P.O. Box 5076, Champaign, IL 61825-5076
1-800-747-4457

Canada: Human Kinetics, Box 24040, Windsor, ON N8Y 4Y9
1-800-465-7301 (in Canada only)

Europe: Human Kinetics, P.O. Box IW14, Leeds LS16 6TR, England
0532-781708

Australia: Human Kinetics, P.O. Box 80, Kingswood 5062, South Australia
618-374-0433

New Zealand: Human Kinetics, P.O. Box 105-231, Auckland 1
(09) 309-2259

To Bob Epskamp,
friend and coach

Contents

Chapter 7 The Essense of Philosopher Coaching 157

Foreword

Beyond Winning provides true insight into the lives of some of our greatest coaches, revealing them not simply as masters of their sport, but as champions of wisdom and understanding as well. Gary Walton's selection and portrayal of Vince Lombardi, Woody Hayes, John Wooden, James "Doc" Counsilman, Brutus Hamilton, and Percy Cerutty has legitimized a new term in athletics: the philosopher coach. Here are six of the most successful personalities who made a lasting impact, not only in the world of sports, but also in the fields of teaching, psychology, planning, and organization. Each one would have been at home in the company of the ancient sages and modern day leaders and scholars.

Each of the coaches is a study in competitive zeal and dedication. Each one shows a fiery passion for his work and an unflagging commitment to excellence. These men have set a standard in combining relentless force with intellectual integrity. This work affords enjoyable reading with revealing examples and formulas for success. As a fellow coach, I give *Beyond Winning* the highest possible endorsement.

——Bill Walsh

Preface:
Signing On
and Getting Competitive

All coaches seek the elusive win, employing as many aspects of sport science and sport superstition as they can muster. Strangely enough, though, some of the winningest coaches have been neither scientists nor shamans: They were philosophers, people of learning and wisdom.

Philosopher coaches are modern sport's answer to the ancient philosopher kings. For these coaches, philosophy and sport are not mutually exclusive. Indeed they are one and the same. To coach is to believe in something: the game, the athlete, the quest for excellence, the process of challenging one's self and striving to overcome. For philosopher coaches, a valiantly fought defeat is better than a poorly played win. Indeed, people's misperception of philosopher coaches is clear in the perennial misquote of Vince Lombardi, who did not say, "Winning isn't everything, it's the only thing," but rather, "Winning isn't everything—but making the effort to win is."

Vince Lombardi, Woody Hayes, John Wooden, Brutus Hamilton, Percy Cerutty, and James "Doc" Counsilman were philosopher coaches who knew the art of winning. As strategic thinkers and tacticians they had few equals. Lombardi, Hayes, Wooden, and Hamilton could have victoriously commanded an army or profitably run a corporation. Cerutty and Counsilman could transform people and inspire them to dazzling heights of achievement. All of them were leaders, men of wisdom, vision, and commitment.

The athletes of these coaches were blessed with state of the art training techniques and both team and personal guidance, but their principal rewards were a deeper perspective on life, on people and organizations, and on themselves. It was these coaches' lessons on team building, preparing for competition, and individual motivation that primarily set them apart and command our attention. With all due respect for their win-loss records—such as Wooden's unbelievable culmination of 10 NCAA national basketball championships in the 1960s and 1970s—these are, after all, just interesting statistics and a rock solid source of engaging conversation. The greater gifts of these men and the lessons we can gain from them are more subtle and harder to preserve. Unless these gifts are brought into a perspective of wider application, they are in danger of being lost forever.

Managers and administrators especially can benefit from the study of men who knew the art of winning with teams and individuals. Above all, these philosopher coaches were experts on people, on "reading them," and on motivating and fitting them together to engage as a team in competition at its best. And certainly every organization, either in government or in business, is better to the extent it functions as a team. Indeed, corporate leaders, statesmen, middle managers, scholars, and aspiring individuals of all types can gain great insight and inspiration from these giants among history's coaching elite.

It is important at the outset, however, to recognize that their teachings offer no simple (or even complicated) formula for getting rich. Like it or not, these stories about hard work, commitment, guts, confidence, loyalty, and princely behavior do not offer an exploitable money-making formula.* But they do reveal wisdom

---

*Indeed, as Professor Donald McCloskey ("The Limits of Expertise: If You're So Smart Why Ain't You Rich?" *The American Scholar*, Summer, 1988, pp. 393-406) has brilliantly and amusingly shown us, there is no common sense to the claim that one person will teach another how to get rich. Common sense guards most of us against the something for nothing advice, or more accurately, the big gain for a small fee deal. Any tip that would advantage you or me, one worth paying for, would also advantage others, including the seller. Why wouldn't the seller exploit the advantage fully? Generosity perhaps? Okay, but if the seller keeps selling the tip, trick, formula, or scheme, it becomes common knowledge and widely used. The news that $500 or $100,000 can easily be made, legally, will draw a rush of buyers for the tip on how to pull it off. As we all use the tip, however, the special advantages that perhaps made the tip initially valuable are lost, driving the value of the tip to zero.

and benchmarks for building leadership talent. Their stories also are a source of inspiration to those aspiring to positions of leadership and management, and to those who want to make a difference in their work, in their community, or in their pursuits, whatever they may be. For some, the goals may be humble—how to better coach the local little league baseball team, revitalize the local Parent Teacher Association, or improve their child's manners. Others may want a promotion, or to get elected mayor. Whatever it is, the impossible has been done many, many times as the philosopher coach knows so well. And one step towards achieving such goals lies in the development of a competitive spirit.

Lombardi, Wooden, Hayes, Counsilman, and Hamilton were all part of a generation of Americans who enjoyed a historical period of unmatched American supremacy after World War II. They and many other leaders of that era were instinctively competitive people who took on the challenges of their times with a passion. Nevertheless, that supremacy ebbed with time.

On February 8, 1967, Lombardi (quoted in "A Coach of Champions: Advice to Businessmen on How to Lead," *U.S. News and World Report*, February 20) spoke to the American Management Association's annual personnel conference. On that occasion, he told over 1,000 corporate executives that

> "Once more we need to develop in this country a strong spirit of competitive interest. We fail in our obligation unless we preserve what has always been an American zeal—that is, to win and to be first, regardless of what we do. . . .

> "What is leadership? It's the ability to direct people. But, more important, to have those people so directed accept it. . . . If you look at management objectively, I think its big trouble is its lack of leadership. . . .

> "I think it is obvious that the difference between the group and the leader is not so much in lack of strength, not so much in lack of knowledge, but rather in lack of will. . . . Unless you maintain discipline, unless you enforce it in a perfect manner, I think you're a potential failure at your job." (p. 14)

Despite his advice, economic events at home and abroad continue to unfold negatively for many American producers. The nation's annual trade deficits hovered at record levels in the 1980s, and the flip from creditor to debtor status in that decade leaves little doubt that American products were being beat to the punch in both domestic and overseas markets. By the 1990s America's international competitiveness in the world stood in stark contrast to its total dominance just four decades earlier.

America's failure in many markets of international competition has been recognized for nearly two decades, and answers to the competitiveness problem abound. Tom Peters, noted author and commentator, argues that America's business schools aren't keeping pace with a changing world. Numerous congressional representatives and senators press for higher tariffs and other protectionist legislation. The eminent management scholar Peter Drucker admonishes managers to recognize that the world has fundamentally changed and that the world economy leads rather than follows any nation's domestic economic policies. Therefore, it is all the more important that individual businesses commit themselves to strategies based on recognition of international competitive forces.

The philosopher coach's thesis is that our stature as a nation depends fundamentally on the strength and character of our people, not on our MBA programs, trade policies, business acumen, or number of engineers, important though they are. It is contended that President Eisenhower's advice on competition is relevant still: "What we are at home and what we do at home is even more important than what we say abroad." It's the old adage in new garb: First, put your house in order.

Beyond Winning is about great coaches who put their houses in order and strengthened the world around them in doing so. These were people who knew the truth of Abe Lincoln's words: "When I do good I feel good; when I don't do good I don't feel good." And they lived life fully, knowing as Arnold Palmer has said, that "if you're not competing, you're dead."

A Personal Note. From 1981 to 1988, it was my pleasure to serve as the first permanent Dean of the Graduate School of Management at the University of California, Davis, and to regularly interact with many leaders from business and government. One of the school's distinguished advisers was C.B. Sung, Chairman of Unison Group Inc., a company that specializes in international business. One afternoon, C.B. provided me with some thought-provoking advice of international dimensions. He said, "You really ought to try and train leaders in your school. You know that's what the Japanese have done. They've been training leaders—and somehow along the way they've made money too." Advice like C.B.'s gives deans sleepless nights. What are the formulas and exercises that mold leaders? What potential do we look for? At what age should we begin training?

If leadership formulas do exist, they are at best vague and untidy, as many books on leadership make painfully clear. Nevertheless, individually and collectively we can make a difference in our community, the nation, and the world, if we commit ourselves to the objective of becoming stronger—physically, mentally, socially, and spiritually. A balanced path of development in each of these areas is one formula for leadership development. I first heard it from my first philosopher coach, Arch Watson, who implored us runners at Sacramento High School to think of our life as the creation of strength. The strongest thing built by man, he said, was the pyramid: three sides (mental, physical, social) and a base (moral or spiritual). Keep each in balance, he advised, and build them up.

As Arch and later Brutus Hamilton at the University of California taught me, winners are people who can rebound from setbacks. Take Clark Kerr, for example, who during the turmoil and campus unrest of the late 1960s came under mounting pressure to resign as the President of the University of California. Upon leaving the fateful meeting of the UC Board of Regents, he candidly announced that he left the job as he took it: "fired with enthusiasm." Undaunted, he charged forward, became Chairman of the Carnegie Commission on Higher Education, and sustained his recognition as one of the greatest educators of all time.

I have enjoyed many conversations with Kerr, ranging from his role in designing the master plan for higher education in California, to the character building he received from running cross-country and track as an undergraduate at Swarthmore. Like other great leaders, he recognizes and appreciates the lessons of athletic competition.

Although the health value of exercise is increasingly recognized and appreciated, absent from the accumulated knowledge in our encyclopedias is the wisdom of the athletic world. It is the intent of *Beyond Winning* to expose the world of conventional learning to the common sense advice of gifted philosopher coaches. Like philosopher kings, these are the sages from the world of athletics. In this new context, the remarkable achievements of the six coaches selected here (and others as well) will take on added significance, buttressed by the value of their wisdom. Student athletes past, present, and future who are in decision-making positions or aspire to them will especially gain from the philosopher coaches' insight, example, and counsel.

Chapter 1

Vince Lombardi:
Demanding Excellence
From His Teams

Picking Lombardi

When the American Management Association (AMA) asked Vince Lombardi to speak to their 1967 annual personnel conference on the topic of what's wrong today in the fields of business and government, no one there questioned the association's reasoning. It mattered not to the listeners that he had no experience in government and only a few years of experience in business as a general manager, in combination with his duties as coach, of the

Vince Lombardi yelling to support his team.

Green Bay Packers. The audience knew that in personnel matters there were few men to rival the likes of Lombardi. He knew human nature, how to lead and manage people.

The problem today (1967) he told the executives, is " 'lack of leadership' "—we need to develop a " 'spirit of competitive interest' " ("A Coach of Champions," p. 14). And the executives listened, because Lombardi's reputation as the Dean of Champions was part of his vintage American winner image. As doleful intellectuals of the era discussed the day's maladies and prospects of decline, Lombardi was telling all who would listen that all things in life are possible if we have faith, dedication, discipline, pride, and total commitment!

As he told the AMA gathering, the main distinction between leaders and followers is not strength or knowledge, but *will*—the zeal to win. For Lombardi, winning was a matter of determination, and Lombardi was a relentlessly determined man.

Like other organizations of the late 60s, the AMA wanted to turn America around and get it moving again. Lombardi was a sound choice for guidance on the problem. Even today, anyone facing the challenges of building a new management team or reorganizing after a takeover would gain from Vince Lombardi's exemplary turnaround of the Green Bay Packers. Lombardi, like few others, really knew how to handle a takeover turnaround challenge.*

The Takeover Turnaround Challenge

Lombardi's turnaround of the bottom-dragging Green Bay Packers crowned his coaching career and earned him the reputation as the best pro football coach in the world, as related by Smith (1962). Between 1948 and 1958, the Green Bay Packers lost more games each season than they won, brought in and spit out three head coaches, and suffered near financial ruin.

In 1958, the Packers hit bottom—winning only one game, tieing another, and losing ten. The 1958 Packers team was nicknamed after a popular dance in the 50s as the La Conga team: Upon each possession it was "one, two, three—kick." Among football

---

*Another is Bill Walsh, whose dramatic and comparable turnaround of the San Francisco 49ers made them the team of the 1980s. The story is told in his new book, with Glenn Dickey, *Building a Champion* (New York: St. Martin's Press, 1990).

enthusiasts, Green Bay became known as Siberia, the place where coaches threatened to send players who missed blocks, fumbled balls, or dropped passes. The daughter of the Packers's center Jim Ringo asked her dad one day, after she'd been harassed at school, "Daddy, are you a bum?" To stop callers with the same question, Ringo had his phone disconnected. Continued torment at school eventually forced the Ringos to take their daughter out of school. The La Conga team was so harassed they socialized with their wives by square dancing in the one safe place for them in town—the locker room.

The first thing Lombardi said upon arrival in Green Bay was that he was no miracle man, but the 1959 team, to risk an understatement, was different. The first thing Lombardi did was to study game films, over and over, in order to decide who to hold on to, who to let go, and how to use the men who were left. A few sagacious trades strengthened the team, but it wasn't the names that changed so much as it was the people. Lombardi's Packers were mostly the same unsung and much maligned personnel he had inherited. Paul Hornung, the All-American "Golden Boy" from Notre Dame, had become the Packers's "Golden Flop." Lombardi chose him for his halfback and told him to live up to his talents. Hornung later noted: " 'Before Lombardi arrived I was a jumping jack—once I was a quarterback, then a fullback. I never knew where I might end up. When he came everything changed. He said, "You're going to be my left halfback, period." Having a coach's backing was like coming out of the dark' " (Moritz, 1963, p. 246).

Third-string quarterback Bart Starr was elevated to the starting role. Lombardi pumped so much confidence into Starr that he became a consummate field general, and Jim Taylor, another unnoticed player, became a national idol at fullback. Hornung, "The Golden Boy," was reborn and won the NFL scoring title three years running.

Lombardi worked on both the minds and bodies of the players. His rules were stringent: Everyone would be on time for meals, meetings, workouts. As the players soon discovered, there was Central time (the zone) and Lombardi time. Lombardi time was fifteen minutes ahead of the clock; woe be it to those who followed only the clock.

Training camp had an eleven o'clock curfew—a rule hated most by the fast-living Hornung. But Lombardi admonished them, "this is a violent sport . . . to play in this league, you've got to be tough—physically tough and mentally tough" (Moritz, 1963, p. 246). And the workouts *were* tough. Dave "Hog" Hanner, who had reported to camp in 1959 weighing 273 pounds, lost so much weight the first three days he had to be hospitalized for dizzy spells.

Lombardi preached and bellowed at the players: " 'Fatigue makes cowards of us all. . . . The harder you work, the harder it is to surrender. . . . If you quit now, during these workouts, you'll quit in the middle of the season, during a game. Once you learn to quit, it becomes a habit. We don't want anyone here who'll quit' " (Kramer, 1968, p. 26). He drove them all with inspiring themes: "spartanism," "total dedication," "winning, it's a habit, you know." His most famous but inaccurately quoted quip, "Winning isn't everything, it's the only thing," failed to convey his belief that mental attitude is 75 percent of winning. But his words as he really stated them did: "Winning isn't everything—but making the effort to win is." Bart Starr (1967, p. 31) called it "Lombardi's philosophy."

How this misstatement occurred is not so puzzling.* As Jerry Kramer concurred with me, "When Vince used 'Winning is the only thing,' he didn't anticipate that a stone cutter would etch it in a tablet and that it would survive until today. Instead, he was talking in a locker room setting, and it was only a statement at that particular moment. It was not his philosophy for the long haul" (personal communication, March 1991).

It was primarily Lombardi's inspiration and drive that set him apart from other men. By his third week with the Packers Lombardi had lost his voice, and there was an emerging crisis in the equipment room; the players had lost so much weight that their game uniforms, ordered at last year's sizes, didn't fit. Rush orders for new pants were made barely in time for the season opener. By then, Lombardi had the best conditioned team in NFL history.

In successive weeks, the Packers opened up by beating the Chicago Bears, the Detroit Lions, and the San Francisco 49ers. They completed 1959 with a 7-5 record, and Lombardi was named NFL coach of the year. In 1960 the Packers won the Western Division title; they lost to Philadelphia in the NFL championship game by only four points. They were the NFL champions in 1961 and 1962,

---

*For Lombardi's personal correction of this quote, see *Vince Lombardi on Football* by G. Flynn (Ed.), p. 16, and *Quarterbacking* by B. Starr, p. 31.

and the first team to win three championships in succession, in 1965, 1966, and 1967. They also won the first two Super Bowl games (1966 and 1967). When Lombardi, at the age of 55, retired from coaching the Packers in 1968, the turnaround team of all time had an astounding win-loss-tie record of 99-29-4.

No Gimmicks

From today's perspective of a high tech world of computers, robotics, and lasers, it may be surprising to learn that Lombardi's competitive edge was not based on technological superiority. No ingenious breakthroughs in football strategies or tactics explain his team's performances. There were no gimmicks, no special plays. His game plan book was thin. Nor did he, as noted earlier, make sweeping personnel changes among the players. Lombardi did recognize the Packers's leadership problem and clearly knew that the key to a successful turnaround was good management by the new people at the top.

Vince Lombardi heading for the locker room with his game plan in hand.

The management situation Lombardi took over was an organizational nightmare. The team had been run by 45 directors statewide. Everyone was in charge, meaning no one, and decisions just weren't getting made. To correct this, Lombardi demanded absolute authority over the team: the power to hire, fire, set standards, pick the uniforms—if he named it he got it. He knew that the link between responsibility and authority is vital to confidence building. The players had to be assured someone was in charge. He put it this way: " 'The strength of the group is in the strength of the leader. Many mornings when I am worried or depressed, I have to give myself what is almost a pep talk, because I am not going before that ball club without being able to exude assurance. I must be the first believer, because there is no way you can hoodwink the players' " (Kramer, 1972, p. x). As the players gained confidence in him, they also gained confidence in themselves, both as individuals and as a team.

Lombardi led by his example of mental toughness which he believed led to physical toughness. He recalls his feelings as head coach after the opening day of practice at Green Bay:

"When I walked back into the locker room, I wanted to cry. The lackadaisical, almost passive attitude was like an insidious disease that had infected the whole squad.

"The next day there were almost twenty players in the trainer's room waiting for diathermy or the whirlpool or a rubdown. I blew my stack.

" 'What is this?' I yelled, 'an emergency casualty ward? Get this straight! When you're hurt, you have every right to be here. But this is disgraceful. I have no patience with the small hurts, play with small hurts, if you're going to play for me.'

"The next day when I walked into that room there were only two players there. So maybe that's how you start building mental toughness. And later on, as our success continued, our mental toughness kept us going in games that looked impossible to win. And the many hurts now seem a small price to have paid for winning." (Flynn, 1973, p. 14)*

---

*Lombardi's own toughness was revealed while he was a player at Fordham: He took 30 stitches in his mouth after playing the whole game against Pittsburgh (Lombardi & Cohane, 1961, p. 105).

A Block of Granite With Brains

There was a solid basis to Lombardi's tough guy reputation. When he played collegiate football at Fordham University, he was a 185-pound guard and one of the famed "Seven Blocks of Granite," as the Fordham linemen were popularly known. However, his emphasis on mental toughness, and indeed his entire approach to the game were developed primarily during his days at West Point where he served as an assistant coach to his beloved mentor Earl "Red" Blaik. Spartanism and total dedication were themes he borrowed from Colonel Blaik. So was Lombardi's emphasis on basics. As he often said, " 'Some people try to find things in this game or put things into it which don't exist. Football is two things. It's blocking and tackling. I don't care anything about formations or new offenses or tricks on defense. You block and tackle better than the team you're playing, you win' " (Maule, 1962, p. 17).

Many who played for and knew Lombardi would be amused by his words, for although the essence of his message is clear, perhaps even correct, he was a *perfectionist* who demanded *total dedication* to improving every aspect of the game. As Lombardi knew, perfection, even in football, demands more than granite toughness, and Lombardi was more than merely tough. He was also an educated man.

Lombardi graduated from Fordham magna cum laude and continued his studies at night at Fordham Law School. In 1939, he launched his coaching career as an assistant football coach at St. Cecilia High School in Englewood Cliffs, New Jersey; in addition to his football coaching responsibilities, and helping coach other sports, he taught Latin, algebra, physics, and chemistry.

Although Lombardi was a dedicated teacher, in 1947 he accepted the freshman football coaching position at Fordham. Then he moved again in 1949 when he grabbed the chance to be Blaik's assistant coach at Army. Blaik, like Lombardi later, had earned a reputation for making something out of nothing. Lombardi called his opportunity to coach alongside Blaik, " 'The most important thing that ever happened to me in football' " (Kramer, 1972, p. 35).

What Lombardi learned from Blaik and football was more than diagrams and techniques. He learned about life.

"To achieve success, whatever the job we have, we must pay a price for success. It's like anything worthwhile. It has a price. You have to pay the price to win and you have to pay the price to get to the point where success is possible. Most important, you must pay the price to stay there. Success is not a 'sometimes' thing. In other words, you don't do what is right once in a while, but all the time. Success is a habit. Winning is a habit.

"Unfortunately, so is losing." (Kramer, 1972, p. 35)

Lombardi preached that in football the price of success was high, and he believed that it was his job as coach to make the price clear. When that was done, and you agreed on the price, then you could forget it and get on with the work. Bart Starr (1967), learned the lesson quickly:

From the time Lombardi first came to Green Bay, along with his staff, it was quite apparent that this was going to be a thoroughly disciplined ball club, highly prepared, mentally and physically tough, and ready to pay whatever price necessary to become champions. You knew immediately that Lombardi was a dedicated individual, sincere and possessed of a burning desire to succeed, and that he would accept nothing less than the best effort of everyone. As a result, I think every one of us on that squad began to push ourselves into utilizing our full capabilities right from the beginning. We knew this man would settle for nothing less than our maximum, and we automatically reacted accordingly. (p. 33)

To build winners, according to Lombardi, " 'you must recognize what has to be done, and then try to do it. It's a matter of recognition, adjustment, and execution, in that order' " (Wind, 1962, pp. 227-228). He delivered on his words. He recognized the talents in his men, made the necessary adjustments in assignments, taught them basic skills, and motivated them.

Motivating and Relating

When asked how Lombardi motivated them, the players most often referred to pride. Gary Knafele, an offensive end, claimed " 'It [pride] made us do things we didn't know we could do. I didn't know I could block. I'd never done it before. He made me a tight end. Then I was ashamed for not having done it before' " (Smith, 1962, p. 52). And it was pride that drove center Jim Ringo to insist

Vince Lombardi at the Superbowl.

on starting against Cleveland in 1961; suffering from 14 painful boils, he made the trainer freeze them just before the game. So outstanding was his performance in their 49-17 victory over the Browns, that he received the highest postgame marks ever handed out by Lombardi and the coaching staff.

Postgame marks were an innovation instituted by Lombardi to generate pride and to allow timely feedback on performances. The outstanding success of this innovation is legendary. The men elbowed each other to get to the mark board first, so anxious were they to receive Lombardi's approval. Frank Gifford, the spectacular halfback of the New York Giants in the mid 1950s when Lombardi was their offensive coach, said, " 'When we played a game I couldn't have cared less about the headlines on Monday. All I wanted was to be able to walk into the meeting Tuesday morning and have Vinny give me that big grin' " (Kramer, 1972, p. 59). By installing pride in performance, Lombardi got proud performances. It's a stagnant manager who simply pays for what he gets, and Lombardi got more out of his players than he paid for, and they got more out of playing than their pay.

Part of the pride was simply being able to cope, for with Lombardi the "whip" was almost always out. He yelled, he screamed, he turned monsters into mice and then transformed them back into even greater monsters than before. The toughest days for the players usually came early in the season and early in the week. By Thursday, Lombardi often would back off and provide some praise and confidence building to send the men into the games on Sunday with a winning attitude. Likewise, near the season's end with the physical work mostly done, he focused on their pride and confidence as professionals and as champions.

Sometimes it appeared that Lombardi was doing a one-man version of "bad cop, good cop." Jerry Kramer (1968) tells of an experience from his first year with Lombardi:

> In 1959, his first year, he drove me unmercifully during the two-a-days. He called me an old cow one afternoon and said that I was the worst guard he'd ever seen. I'd been working hard, killing myself, and he took all the air out of me. I'd lost seven or eight pounds that day, and when I got into the locker room, I was too drained to take my pads off. I just sat in front of my locker, my helmet off, my head down, wondering what I was doing playing football, being as bad as I was, getting cussed like I was. Vince came in and walked over to me, put his hand on the back of my head, mussed my hair and said, "Son, one of these days you're going to be the greatest guard in the league." He is a beautiful psychologist. I was ready to go back out to practice for another four hours. (pp. 78-79)

In short Lombardi usually reversed the management canon of praising publicly and chewing out privately.

Lombardi cared deeply for all his players and would not tolerate any form of prejudice or special privilege. When Lombardi first arrived in Green Bay in 1959, Nate Borden was the only Black on the team. Borden was renting a place described as unfit for a dog. When Lombardi found out, he gave the owners hell and found Borden a decent place to live. According to Emlen Tunnell, a Black who came from the Giants with Lombardi that same year, Lombardi told the team on the first day of practice: " 'If I ever hear of anyone using any racial epithets around here, like Nigger or Dago or Jew, you're gone. I don't care who you are' " (Kramer, 1972, p. 72).

Shortly into Lombardi's first season as head coach, the Packers traveled to the South for an exhibition game. The hotels had already been booked with separate accommodations by race. Lombardi was stuck with the arrangements, but when the restaurant told him the "Negro players" had to enter and leave by the back door, he had every member of the team enter and leave together through the back door. The next year when they went south, the team all stayed and ate together on a nearby air force base (Kramer, 1968, p. 27).

Lombardi was truly free of racial prejudice. One of the most famous quips about Lombardi, made by defensive tackle Henry Jordan, indicated the coach's consistent fairness: " 'He treats us all the same. Like dogs' " ("A Team for All Time," 1970, p. 62).

Lombardi wanted togetherness and wouldn't tolerate shirkers, special privileges, or cliques, either among the players or their wives. He insisted on perfection, together, from everyone. Sometimes he pushed this to uncomfortable extremes, as Jerry Kramer (1968) recalls.

> Marie Lombardi [the coach's wife] joined us at a team dinner before one game last year, and the dessert was apple pie. Marie asked the waiter if she could have a scoop of ice cream on her pie, and before the waiter could answer, Vince jumped out of his seat, red in the face, and bellowed, "When you travel with the team, and you eat with the team, you eat what the team eats." (pp. 27-28)

Whether it was singing, to lighten the spirit and raise team morale, or saying the Lord's prayer, which the team did before and after every game, it was done by all the Packers together. The quality of the voice did not matter, and sinners and devout were treated equally. They were all Packers—Lombardi men.

Final Sparks

About a year after Lombardi quit as coach to devote himself full time to the general manager duties of the Packers, he said,

> "When I quit, I *knew* I'd never be back coaching. I *knew* I wouldn't be able to take it again. The pressures were so horrible. You know, the pressure of losing is bad, awful, because it kills you eventually. But the pressure of winning is worse, infinitely worse, because it keeps on torturing you and torturing you and torturing you. At Green Bay, I was winning one championship after another, after another, after another. I couldn't take it, because I blamed myself, damned myself

whenever they lost a game. I couldn't ever forgive myself for a loss, because I felt I'd let them down." (Johnson, 1969, p. 30)

Within weeks of his decision to step aside as coach, however, the signs of discontent were already apparent. He said he didn't " 'miss the meetings and the practices. . . . I don't miss any of that. . . . First of all, I miss the rapport with the players. I was close to them and they to me. . . . I miss the fire on Sundays' " (Heinz, 1968, p. 121).

In 1969, with a new objective in mind, he elaborated:

"What I missed most was—well, it wasn't the tension and the crowds and the game on Sunday. And it certainly wasn't the winning. And it wasn't the spotlight and all that. . . . There's a great . . . closeness on a football team, you know—a rapport between the men and the coach that's like no other sport. It's a binding together, a knitting together. For me, it's like father and sons, and that's what I missed. I missed players coming up to me and saying, 'Coach, I need some help because my baby's sick.' or, 'Mr. Lombardi, I want to talk to you about trouble I'm having with my wife.' That's what I missed most. The closeness." (Johnson, 1969, p. 33)

The Lombardi era at Green Bay was once described as "a comet burned out by the heat of its own brilliance" (Johnson, 1969, p. 33), but there were final sparks yet to come.

Perhaps to confound any possible skeptics, Lombardi would launch a repeat turnaround performance in 1969. Bored as general manager at Green Bay and missing the closeness of the men, he accepted the head coach position for the Washington Redskins. The Redskins hadn't put a winning season together in 14 years. Lombardi made sure it wasn't 15. He transformed a dispirited bunch of losers into winners, marshaling an impressive 7-5-2 record. His approach was essentially the same: the basics, with confidence and pride. That was his legacy to football and to life.

Lombardi's first words to the press upon arrival in Washington, DC were characteristically Lombardi: " 'Gentlemen, it is not true that I can walk across the Potomac River . . . not even when it's frozen' " (Johnson, 1969, p. 29). Lombardi's effect on the players was also characteristically Lombardi. Ray McDonald, a large, young fullback who had been having problems adapting to the pros said,

"I'd do those grass drills all day for The Man. I'd run till I dropped. I'd do anything for him. He told us we had to love one another, to care for other players on the team if we were going to *be* a team. He's a genius, a *genius*. We had a one-hour meeting last night. You know how many plays he gave us? Two. Only two plays in one hour. But we saw those plays like we never saw plays before." (Underwood, 1969, p. 18)

Sonny Jurgensen, the Redskins's great quarterback, had been on the verge of quitting. He was 34 years old and tired of losing, despite personal glory.

"I saw myself as a man who had applied himself diligently to professional football for 12 years," he said, "and never really got the most out of it. I saw them as frustrating years. I was up to here with records. What did they mean? Nothing. One year I threw 508 passes. One year I threw 32 touchdown passes. But we never won anything.

"It seemed all I could look forward to year after year was drop back and throw, drop back and throw, much of the time in sheer fright, but usually because there was no other way. Not winning, just throwing. I always felt I had my back to the wall. It was always second and eight. We were always disorganized. We were always making up plays in the huddle." (Underwood, 1969, p. 20)

Right after the announcement about Lombardi, the fast-living Jurgensen immediately phoned the fast-living Hornung. Hornung told him " 'Sonny, don't worry about a thing. You'll love him. Forget everything else you've ever heard. You'll *love* Vince Lombardi. He'll be fair, and it'll be a whole new deal for you. Look, I played for him, didn't I?' " (Underwood, 1969, p. 20). Hornung's words would prove prophetic. Jurgensen, along with several teammates, attended a four-day meeting that June with their new coach, Lombardi. Afterwards, Jurgensen declared himself astounded by Lombardi's grasp of the game: " 'His passing game amazes me, the science of it. The consistency of it' " (Underwood, 1969, p. 20). He found himself eagerly anticipating training camp; to the astonishment of his fellow players, Jurgensen arrived with not only a conservative haircut, but also a much trimmer waistline. Indeed, Jurgensen had adopted a whole new style and attitude.

Tackle Ray Schoenke recalls this early impression in training camp: "Coach Lombardi had just put us through this long, agonizing grass drill. We were about to drop when suddenly he yells for Sonny and Sam Huff to lead us three laps around the field. I'll never forget it. Sonny looks at Huff and says 'If *you* can do it so can I' and they're *grinning!* All us young guys who were thinking we couldn't take any more felt pretty silly." (Cartwright, 1969, p. 50)

What was different about the new Redskins? Lombardi called it "mental toughness."

Lombardi and Success

Dedication, desire, pride in performance, confidence, and teaching ability are the words and thoughts that flow from those who knew and worked with Lombardi when they ponder his many contributions to football and life. Some will argue that it was primarily his inspirational personality that set Lombardi apart from others. Red Smith, in his foreword to *Vince Lombardi on Football* (Flynn, 1973), starts with one of his many personal encounters with Lombardi.

In a tower suite in Milwaukee's Hotel Pfister, Vince Lombardi sat chatting with half a dozen sportswriters on the afternoon of Dec. 22, 1967. In something like 20 hours the Green Bay Packers would go after their third straight championship of the National Football League's Western Conference, playing the Los Angeles Rams, who had upset them two Sundays earlier. As relaxed as he ever could be on the eve of a game, the coach held forth on the theme that was the core of his existence—the commitment to excellence and to victory.

"As St. Paul wrote in one of the Epistles," he said, " 'Know ye not that they which run in a race run all, but one receiveth the prize? So run, that ye may obtain.' "

. . .

"How about that?" a man said in the corridor outside. "St. Vincent de Paul!"

"The Gospel according to Lombardi," another said.

They scattered to their own rooms to check chapter and verse in the Gideon Bibles. The man had it right.

"Vince has a knack," the Packers' all-pro guard, Jerry Kramer, said later, "for making all the saints sound like they would have been great football coaches."

I don't know why this incident keeps coming back to mind unless it is because it illustrates the paradox that was the essence of Vince Lombardi—a deeply religious man who worshipped the God of peace and taught a game of cruel violence, with total dedication to both.

George Flynn (1973), a close friend of Lombardi who worked closely with him on books and the film series *Vince Lombardi's Science and Art of Football*, claims in his foreword:

Vince Lombardi's success, I am convinced, lay not only in his inspirational personality but also in his ability to *teach*. He was a teacher. He could communicate an idea to his players, explain it so that they understood it—not only how to execute it but why! He taught, right to the heart of the matter, without frills or gimmicks. You had to be smart to play for Lombardi. In a split second a lineman had to read and react to the move of his opponent, and react correctly—so for all players, both offense and defense. Of course the physical talent was there, but all teams in professional football have that. The ability of his teams to do the right thing—cut the right way, block the right man, read the key correctly—these are the reasons for the championships.

Few men knew Lombardi, his complexity and moods, like Bart Starr. Starr spent a lot of time with him, hellish stressful moments as well as moments of triumph. As Starr says,

"Lombardi felt that every fiber in your body should be used in an effort to seek excellence, and he sought this goal every day of his life with complete dedication. He stated this thought eloquently to us one day in a meeting: 'The quality of a man's life is in direct proportion to his commitment to excellence, regardless of his chosen field or endeavor.'

"I considered this to be the finest statement he ever made to the Packer squad. It is typical of the man: direct, sharp, inspirational, encompassing. Notice the word 'football' is not mentioned. He never treated football as an end result, but rather a means to an end. He was concerned with the full, total life. It emphasizes his commitment and flaming desire to excel. He was tough on his players because he was tough on himself. He never expected more from us than he was willing to give of himself. He would not tolerate excuses or compromises, but was interested only in results. Tough, demanding, abrasive, he was also compassionate and understanding. For though he recognized that absolute perfection is never attainable, he believed the quest for it can be one of the most challenging races an individual can run." (Flynn, 1973, Foreword)

Lombardi didn't let winning—meeting goals—soften him on essential values of competition. As he put it: " 'The will to excel and the will to win, they endure. They are more important than any events that occasion them' " (Kramer, 1972, p. x).

The Legend

When Lombardi left his offices on Lombardi Avenue in Green Bay for the Redskins's turf on L Street in Washington, DC, the press and capital city residents treated his arrival with unmatched enthusiasm. No other man was more responsible for raising pro football in America to near obsession levels. When asked about the Lombardi Legend, he replied,

"Legend? Well, yeah, I suppose I thought about my legend before I came here," he growled. He scratched his head. He stared fixedly at the floor. He ducked his chin down toward his necktie. He was silent. . . . "Dammit," he finally burst out, "dammit, I'm not a legend, because I don't want to be a legend. One main reason I came back to coaching is that I didn't want to be regarded as a legend. Because one, it's embarrassing as the devil, and two, you have to be Halas to be a legend. George Halas is 74 years old and he's done something for the game. I'm too young to be a legend." (Johnson, 1969, p. 29)

Saint Vincent, as he was sometimes called (though never directly), exuded a strength of character and brute determination that seemed impossible to stop. But on September 3, 1970, the game's greatest coach, aged 57, succumbed to intestinal cancer in Georgetown University Hospital. The invincible Lombardi had become an instant legend—against his will. The philosophical basis of the Lombardi Legend was total dedication to the pursuit of excellence.

As Jerry Kramer (1970), the leading expert on Lombardi and five time All-Pro guard, wrote shortly after his beloved coach's death, "A while ago Frank Gifford was talking about Vince's belief in the Spartan life, the total self-sacrifice. 'You and me—we grew up believing in Lombardi's way of life. I'm not sure that it's the answer for everybody, but I wish my son could play for Vince Lombardi.' " And Jerry thoughtfully added, " 'I do, too' " (p. 54).

Jerry Kramer also provided a near perfect epitaph, with words written in 1967 en route to the Packers's third-straight NFL Championship. " 'I had hated him at times during training camp and I had hated him at times during the season, but I knew how much he had done for us, and I knew how much he cared about us. He is a beautiful man' " (A Special Madness," 1970, p. 123). But Lombardi had his own words: " 'You never lose. But sometimes the clock runs out on you' " (Kramer, 1972, p. 176).

Vince Lombardi's Head Coaching Record

Year	Team	Won	Lost	Tied	Percent (excluding ties)	
1942	St. Cecilia	6	1	2	.857	
1943	St. Cecilia	11	0	0	1.000	
1944	St. Cecilia	10	0	1	1.000	
1945	St. Cecilia	5	3	2	.625	
1946	St. Cecilia	7	3	0	.700	
1959	Green Bay	7	5	0	.583	(Third place)
1960	Green Bay	8	4	0	.667	(Western champions)
1961	Green Bay	11	3	0	.786	(NFL champions)
1962	Green Bay	13	1	0	.929	(NFL champions)
1963	Green Bay	11	2	1	.846	(Second place)
1964	Green Bay	8	5	1	.615	(Second place)
1965	Green Bay	10	3	1	.769	(NFL champions)
1966	Green Bay	12	2	0	.857	(World champions)
1967	Green Bay	9	4	1	.692	(World champions)
1969	Washington	7	5	2	.583	(Second place)
Totals		135	41	11	.767	

His Green Bay teams were 42-8 in preseason games, 10-2 in postseason games.

His Washington team was 2-4 in preseason games.

His overall record: 189 victories, 55 defeats, 11 ties, .775 percent.

From 1939 through 1941, he was an assistant at St. Cecilia High School.

From 1947 through 1948, he was an assistant at Fordham University.

From 1949 through 1953, he was an assistant at West Point.

From 1954 through 1958, he was an assistant with the New York Giants.

Chapter 2

Woody Hayes:
Patton or Plato?

The Media's Villain

When Wayne Woodrow Hayes died on March 12, 1987, the media recounted vivid stories of his legendary triumphs and tragedies as a coach. The coverage was as lively and timely as that of the events surrounding his dismissal for public misconduct. On December 29, 1978, in the final minutes of the Gator Bowl, Charlie Bauman intercepted an Ohio State University pass to preserve Clemson University's narrow lead and assure their victory. As Bauman passed by the OSU sidelines, Woody punched him in the throat. Millions of viewers saw it live on TV, and no one was surprised

Woody Hayes, upset and disturbed, Fall 1971.

by the morning headlines: Woody fired. Fired at age 66 after 28 triumphant years! It adds spice to the story to note that when Woody later called Charlie Bauman on the phone, it wasn't to apologize. He wanted to know what formation Clemson had used on that critical play.

Woody's moments of callousness and ill-temper made great copy, and there was material galore. Just six weeks before the ill-fated Gator Bowl game, Woody was ending a year-long probation imposed by the Big Ten office for taking a swing at ABC photographer Mike Freedman. Hayes sent Freedman and his camera flying, again in full view of a national TV audience watching the battle at Ann Arbor between OSU and Michigan. At the 1973 Rose Bowl, another incident prompted Art Rogers, a *Los Angeles Times* photographer, to charge Hayes with assault (charges later dropped) for intentionally shoving Rogers's camera in his face. In 1971, Woody destroyed an Ann Arbor sideline marker in another temper tantrum over a missed pass interference call—as he saw it—by an official. In 1959, two California reporters accused Woody of throwing punches at them after OSU lost the Rose Bowl to USC. His first big moment of volatility with the press was in 1958, when an invited contingent of sportswriters known as the Big Ten Skywriters, along with Big Ten Commissioner Tug Wilson, were suddenly asked to leave the practice field. Woody hadn't liked the practice and wanted to chew out the team privately. He got his way. No apologies here either; it was Dick Larkins, the athletic director, who later rendered an apology to the commissioner and the press.

Woody's players, fellow coaches, friends, and fans would be the first to agree that his critics had a few valid points. But they would be quick to add that if you knew the whole man, what he stood for and what he did, then his shortcomings faded into insignificance. It is doubly ironic that his firing was for misconduct, because he was a man of self-imposed high principles who effectively maintained strict rules of conduct for his players as well. Hotel managers often commented on the good behavior of Hayes's players at out of town games. In short, Woody was a man of stark contrasts. One would need an accountant's ledger to tally his faults and virtues.

A balanced view doesn't always make good script, however, and Woody-bashing was too popular a national sport, especially on the West Coast, to yield to dispassionate perspectives. One prominent sportswriter for the *Sacramento Bee* went so far as to assert that

Woody all too often "confused football with war" (Hamelin, 1987, p. C-1). By his words Hamelin mistook ignorance for temperament; no one could match Hayes's understanding of the similarities and differences between war and football, as I can personally attest.

I first met Woody one afternoon in 1966 in St. Johns Arena while we were washing our hands in the men's room. He turned and asked me, curiously, what a professorial-looking guy was doing in the gym? I told him I was a professor of economic history and came down daily to run with the distance runners on the track team. He insisted I come to his office—where I received an hour-long lecture on military history, football, leadership, and philosophy. It was a dazzling tour de force, the kind of experience you never forget. Former President Richard Nixon had a similar experience and reaction. He first met Woody in 1957 right after OSU beat Iowa 17-13. Woody was on the brink of his second national championship. Nixon recalled the moments:*

> Afterwards, at a victory reception, John Bricker introduced me to Woody. I wanted to talk about football. Woody wanted to talk about foreign policy. You know Woody—we talked about foreign policy.

> For thirty years thereafter, I was privileged to know the real Woody Hayes—the man behind the media myth. Instead of a know-nothing Neanderthal, I found a renaissance man with a consuming interest in history and a profound understanding of the forces that move the world. Instead of a cold, ruthless tyrant on the football field, I found a warm-hearted softie—very appropriately born on Valentine's Day—who often spoke of his affection for his boys, as he called them, and for his family.

Besides his wisdom and sheer power of conviction, Woody is also personally unforgettable to me because he easily ranks as one of the toughest men I ever met. Except for his last few years of coaching, his routine top garment for games was only a short-sleeved shirt. He wore this even in paralyzingly cold weather purposely to set an example for his players and opponents. The loyal 85,000 fans who sat freezing in coats and blankets in the stands loved every minute of it. Again, it was ironic that his example

---

*Extracted from a speech delivered by Richard M. Nixon at the memorial service for Woody Hayes, Columbus, OH, March 17, 1987.

to others spurred his critics and prompted his dismissal. But there is no denying his bursts of temper, poor sportsmanship, and steadfast refusal to apologize.

Heroes, Ideas, and Values

Hayes was always a self-proclaimed hero worshipper of tough men; Cy Young, Red Grange, Walter Johnson, Gene Tunny, and Knut Rockne were among his earliest heroes. But while majoring in English and history at Denison University, he read Ralph Waldo Emerson's essays, and Emerson catapulted to the top of his list. Through Emerson, Woody discovered a positive philosophy that strongly reinforced the virtues instilled in him by his family. Above all else he ranked self-reliance a top virtue, right along with education. So did his parents who, according to Woody, never bought anything on credit. Late in life and bedridden, Woody's father called him to his side. An unpaid debt was worrying him, and he told Woody about stopping in at Russell Bean's clothing store several days earlier for a new pair of shoes. He'd forgotten his money and the shoes cost $8.50, but Russell gave them to Woody's dad and said he could pay later. As he told Woody, "If something happens to me, Russell will never send a bill. Go pay him 'cause I don't want to leave this world owing anything." Woody paid the debt, and his dad died about a week later.

Woody believed independence and self-reliance were special traits of hill and mountain people like the Montagnards in Vietnam, Tibetans, the folk of West Virginia and Kentucky, and his own relatives in Noble County, the hilliest and least populated area of Ohio. During a visit to his 94-year-old Aunt Bertha in Noble County, he asked her how many offspring she had. She said, "At last count there were 119," and then showing her hill upbringing added, "Not one of them or any of their parents have ever been on welfare." Self-reliance was in his blood, and Emerson's philosophy made him conscious of it. When advising many other coaches seeking his secrets of success, he would always conclude, in Emersonian fashion, "Be yourself, not me."

Hayes's command of scholarly works and his passion for Emerson's writings contrasted totally with the Neanderthal image occasionally portrayed of him by the press. A moment of great personal satisfaction for him and a time of puzzlement for his critics was on

May 2, 1982, when Hayes joined former Attorney General and
Secretary of Defense Elliot Richardson and former Watergate special prosecutor Archibald Cox as keynote speakers at Harvard
University. The event commemorated the life and work of Emerson
on the occasion of the 100th anniversary of his death.

The 69-year-old Hayes, in dark suit, white-haired, wearing
steel rim glasses and a smile on his face, stood on the podium in
the mahogany, century-old, three-tiered auditorium in Sanders
Theater.

"I'm sure you're wondering what a football coach is doing
here tonight," he said.

"It's simple," Hayes said, "I've come to pay back something
I owe." "Emerson," he went on, "was an inspiration to me all
my life—he was a big factor, not the only factor, of course, but
an important one. He wrote about how important spirit and
attitude were. He was an enormously positive man." Hayes
paused, then added, "He would've made a great football
coach." The audience responded with laughter.

The essay, "Compensation," said Hayes, was, for him, the
single most significant work by Emerson. "I've only read it at
least 50 times in the last half century," said Hayes. "My father
gave it to me when I was a college student at Denison, in Ohio.
He told me that Emerson said that the more you give, the more
you get in return. I was charmed by the fancy of this endless
compensation. And doggone if it isn't true.

"It became the cornerstone of my coaching philosophy. I would
quote from it so often that my players would say, 'Oh, no, not
again, coach.' And I'd say, 'Well, then, play football or I will
read it again!' "

And how does a football coach get his players to respond? "I
never talked down to them," said Hayes. "I learned that from
Mr. Emerson. He said, 'Treat men as pawns and ninepins and
you shall suffer as well as they.' I remember one year early in
my coaching career I made that mistake. And we had a terrible
season. I never made that mistake again.

"Even when I thundered at the players, I thundered that they
could do better."

Another crucial point made by Emerson, added Hayes, is that
"Our strength grows out of our weakness. Mr. Emerson,"

Hayes continued, "said that 'the indignation which arms itself with secret forces does not awaken until we are pricked and stung and sorely assailed.'

"After a loss, I'd recite that and tell my players, 'It's us.' " And after victory? "Mr. Emerson said that we should 'beware of too much good staying in your hand. It will fast corrupt and worm worms.' " Hayes shrugged at the worms part. "Well, that's what he said." The audience laughed.

"So when people start congratulating me on winning," Hayes continued, "that's when I want to kick them in the shins. Mr. Emerson said, 'Whilst he sits on the cushion of advantages, he goes to sleep. When he is pushed, tormented, defeated, he has a chance to learn something; he has been put on his wits, his manhood.'

"So we could never take it easy even when we won—especially when we won, and that's one reason we kept winning. We were the only team in the Big 10 to win 17 straight conference games—and we did it two times."

With that, Hayes invoked another philosopher, one from the 20th century. "As Dizzy Dean said, 'If you done it, it ain't braggin.' " (Berkow, 1982, p. C-7)

Woody's brusque, thundering manner only partially hid his soft heart and selfless commitment to others. His weekly visits to hospitals to read and talk with total strangers to cheer them up are legend. However, these and hundreds of other stories of his impromptu assistance to people would only sidetrack us. Here again, the principal influence was Emerson; " 'The one base thing in the universe is to receive favors and render none. In the order of nature, we cannot render benefits to those from whom we receive them or only seldom, but the benefit we receive must be rendered again line for line, deed for deed, cent for cent to somebody. Beware of too much good staying in your hand. . . . Pay it away quickly in some sort' " (cited in Leroux, 1982, p. 4-1). Woody's proud interpretation of this, which set the pattern for his life, was that for the most part we can't pay back all those who have helped us, so we have to *pay forward*. He linked this perspective to his favorite poem, "The Bridge Builder" by William A. Dromgoole, whose words he had riveted to memory.

"An old man going a lone highway
Came at evening cold and grey
To a Chasm vast and wide and steep
With waters rolling cold and deep
. . . .

Good friend, in the path that I have come today
There followeth after me a youth whose feet must
   pass this way
The Chasm that was as naught to me
To that fair haired youth may a pitfall be
He too must pass in the twilight dim.
Good friend, I'm building this bridge for him."

Leadership

Hayes served five years in the Navy during World War II, after enlisting five months *before* Pearl Harbor. He reached the rank of Lt. Commander and served as the commanding officer of the patrol craft *PC1251* in the Palau Islands invasion and of the destroyer escort *Rinehart* in operations in both the Atlantic and Pacific. The experience of war was telling on Woody, and he visited soldiers and officers in Vietnam three times during the U.S. involvement in the war there. In his mind, war, football, history, and daily life were all interwoven. In his speeches and writings, he drew episodic lessons from each. He had a passion for great men and moments in history; he studied them meticulously, but he did not dwell on the past. Hayes lived for tomorrow. The season's victories or defeats were worthy of contemplation only to remind him of the tasks ahead and of the need for continued preparation. Similarly, he studied war and history to gain inspiration and perspective on the main forces of his competitive world. Hayes thrived on challenges and on the preparation for them, and as he often said of his competitors, "They may outsmart me, or be luckier, but they can't out work me" (personal communication, circa 1967).

One military hero who deeply inspired Woody was Sun Tzu. In his book, *The Art of War*, (circa 500 BC), Sun Tzu wrote: " 'All men can see these tactics whereby I conquer, but what none can see is the strategy out of which victory is evolved' " (Hayes, 1969, p. 2).

Woody admired Sun Tzu's special sense of the term strategy. Woody took it to mean a habit of offensive thinking and forward thinking, like his own perspective on paying debts forward. For Woody, strategy emphasized a positive attitude that in more concrete terms meant everything that went into planning *before* the games. Tactics were merely reactive changes made in the games, but strategy was practice, preparation, and planning—offensive, forward thinking.

Hayes fundamentally believed that there was no substitute for careful, thorough preparation; it was his strategy. The following quotations, all emphasizing essentially this same thing, are taken from the beginning of his chapter "Organization and Planning" in *Hot Line to Victory* (1969, p. 271):

- Luck is infatuated with the efficient.—*A Persian Proverb*

- Chance favors the prepared mind.—*Pasteur*

- If I don't practice for one day, I know it, if I don't practice for two days, the CRITICS know it, if I don't practice for three days, EVERYONE knows it.—*Ignace Paderewski, the great Polish pianist*

- Luck is what happens when preparation meets opportunity.—*Coach Darrell Royal*

- The will to win is not nearly as important as the will to prepare to win.—*Anonymous*

- Proper preparation prevents poor performance.—*U.S. Marines*

- Plan your work and work your plan.—*U.S. Army*

To Woody, preparation was also a hallmark of leadership, and he listed it sixth among his 10 virtues and characteristics of a good leader (see Table 2.1). First listed is the ability "to project a *positive image* of initiative, enthusiasm, competitiveness, resolution, character, and integrity," a real mouthful of offensive thinking. Second was the *mental toughness* to withstand pressure and to bounce back from setbacks. As many have argued, the real test of a leader is in times of grave danger, and in that context Lincoln, Roosevelt, and Churchill inspired Hayes the most. So did President Kennedy, who wrote, " 'A man does what he must, in spite of personal consequences, in spite of obstacles and dangers and pressures—and this is the basis of all human morality' " (Hayes, 1969, p. 293).

Table 2.1
Woody's Ten Virtues and Characteristics of a Good Leader

---

1. Positive image, character, and integrity
2. Mental toughness, to endure and rebound
3. Communication skills
4. To not underestimate the role of the leader
5. To know your limits and be yourself
6. Preparation, including anticipation
7. Accessibility and visibility
8. Confidence
9. Ability to initiate interaction
10. To not underestimate the spiritual power of people

Note. From Hayes (1969). Reprinted by permission.

Third on the list was *communication,* and here again Woody would remind us of Churchill's gifted skill to say the right thing, at the right time, in the right way. Upon taking over as Prime Minister of Britain in 1940 shortly after Germany's capture of France, and with an aerial onslaught and possible invasion imminent, Churchill warned his countrymen, "I have nothing to offer but blood, toil, tears, and sweat." To the Germans, he promised

"We shall fight on the seas and oceans, we shall fight with growing confidence and growing strength in the air, we shall defend our island, whatever the cost may be: we shall fight on the beaches, we shall fight on the landing-grounds, we shall fight in the fields and in the streets, we shall fight in the hills; we shall never surrender; and even if, which I do not for a moment believe, this island or a large part of it were subjugated and starving, then our Empire beyond the seas, armed and guarded by the British Fleet, would carry on the struggle, until, in God's good time, the new world, with all its power and might, steps forth to the rescue and the liberation of the old." (Hayes, 1969, p. 294)

Woody's fourth characteristic of leadership was to *not underestimate the role of the leader.* In good times or bad, outcomes will be affected by tenacity and consistency of leadership. His fifth characteristic was to *know your limits and be yourself.* He based it on General Creighton Abrams's reply to a question on the essence of

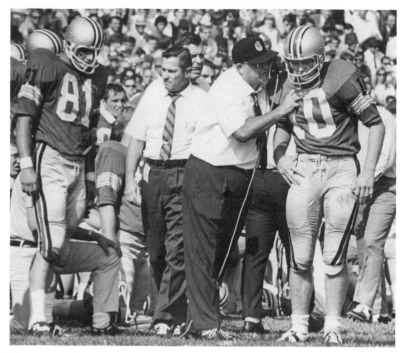

Woody communicating to Rex Kern (10), his quarterback during the OSU vs. Purdue game, October 12, 1968. Richard Kuhn is number 81.

leadership, namely that, "A man must know what he can do, and he must be himself." To pretend or exaggerate one's talents is to invite disrespect. Sixth, as noted, is *preparation, including anticipation*, which together are insurance against surprise. As Woody (1969) said, "It was no accident in the Battle of the Bulge that General Patton was able to relieve Bastogne, for he had anticipated the point of the German break through. His 'mock up,' the enemy strength board, was always with him and always up to the minute" (p. 295). Seventh was *accessibility and visibility*. General Lewis Walt, in reply to a question in Vietnam on rules he lived by, answered, "He who would be first among you, must be the servant to all."

Hayes lists *confidence* eighth, but General Patton had ranked it the most vital quality of a soldier. Hayes (1969) reported that "In 1933, General Patton wrote: 'Wars may be fought with weapons, but they are won with men. It is the spirit of the men who follow and of the man who leads that gains the victory' " (p. 296). Ninth was the ability to *initiate interaction* between leaders and the larger group, and tenth was to not underestimate the *spiritual power* of people. Hitler's folly on this point during the Battle of Britain, at Leningrad, Moscow, and Stalingrad are notched in history. Hayes (1969) also reminds us that General Rommel underestimated the Allied landings in Normandy; "With storms raging up and down the coast of Europe, he reasoned that the Americans would not try an invasion under these conditions, so he went home to celebrate his wife's birthday. The date—June 6, 1944" (p. 296).

Knowing and appreciating people is implicit in the list and is apparent in Woody's descriptions of great leadership. He retold a story of Creighton Abrams who served as a Lt. Colonel under General Patton in the Battle of the Bulge. During their hard-fought drive into Germany, Abrams and other key officers received orders from Patton to meet him at a farm house. Days and nights of continuous battle had been raging, and the request for a meeting caught them all by surprise. So did his words. By Hayes's account, Patton told the officers that he had no further orders for them other than to continue the great job they were doing. He explained that there comes a time when a leader needs his morale strengthened by those with whom he serves. He finished by saying that he had called this meeting so he could be with his comrades-in-arms, to thank them for the great contribution they were making toward the ultimate victory. Hayes (1969) tells us that "General Abrams pointed out that the effect on these officers was electrifying. Here was a leader who had the ability and the thoughtfulness to express with timeliness and warmth his gratitude to the men who deserved the credit—a gesture which is often easily forgotten in the rush of events (p. 295).

Woody was sometimes likened to a genius by his friends and certain members of the press, such as David Condon. But he wouldn't hear of that. He felt that the key to great coaching was great players. Genius or not, Woody was smart enough to know that the quality of a leader is largely measured by the effects of collective effort, and by the quality of a group's subordinate leaders and members. Leaders without followers are impotent; leaders with talentless followers are ineffective.

Organization

Winning with people was basic to Hayes's philosophy and sense of organization. Hard-working, self-reliant, quality people were tops on his list. He selected his fellow coaches first on character, second on personality traits and work habits, and third on technical competence. He reasoned that if he found someone tops in the first two, he could teach them whatever else they needed to know.

He strived to make sure his associates felt part of the organization. He built his program with a *WE* attitude to spur commitment and performance. Mutual respect was essential, and Woody involved others in the decision-making process in hiring. New hires came with the group's blessing, and not just as Woody's picks. He excited newcomers with the fact that they were joining a group of talented, exceptional people dedicated to winning.

Frequent communication, clear specific assignments, routine follow-up, no favoritism, and above all, keeping his word were Woody's trademarks. To insure trust, and the best possible results, he felt the head coach should tell his subordinates what to do, but not how. Deciding how to do an assignment best was their job. Timely feedback, both positive and negative, would suggest changes in methods if any were needed. Woody didn't like to impose rules, and he labored to build up an attitude toward commonly held goals and values to lessen the need for rules. The more successful he was in attracting top people, the more clearly he recognized the inevitability of turnover and the loss of fellow workers to outside opportunities. But Woody believed he should never stand in the way of a coach's promotion. As he saw it, a subordinate's promotion, like that of Bo Schembechler to the head coaching position at the University of Michigan, was a reflection on the quality of the OSU program. It was another way of paying forward, and in giving Woody received. OSU's reputation for fast promotion enhanced his recruiting of coaches and hastened the introduction of new ideas into his ranks.

A strong determined leader with a reputation for temper tan-trums like Woody would instill caution in even the most confident critic, and he knew he would lose the benefit of valuable suggestions and criticism if he didn't work consciously to get them. Woody respected his fellow coaches and showed it. He believed that when a coach came to him with criticism he had better listen intently, for someone with the strength of conviction to volunteer criticism was often right. Secondly, after each spring and fall practice he had each coach write an informal critique of the experience. Then the ideas were discussed in meetings, and improvements were made.

Woody's views on coaching and organization were largely specific applications of his leadership fundamentals. The coach's desire to win must be visible and strong, and it must be a "*WE* win" rather than an "*I* win" attitude. More importantly, he believed the coach must have "an *intense and continuing interest* in the welfare and *all around development* of each player" (1969, p. 279). This set his style of recruiting players. He didn't make promises to the prospective players, but instead praised the athlete's ability and potential and challenged him to become a "Buckeye." For the parents, Woody appealed to their educational interests with stories of his many players' successes in undergraduate, graduate, and professional schools, and beyond. As everyone at OSU knew, Woody didn't just send his players to the study table—he met them there.

These and many other examples of Woody's sincere interest and commitment to his players' development beyond the football field were other ways he paid forward, and again, the more he gave the more he received in return. One of his former players, who became a prominent midwestern neurosurgeon, wrote Hayes shortly after entering Harvard Medical School that he was dropping out. The grind and pressure were too great, and he wanted Woody not to hear of his decision second hand. Within hours, the coach caught a plane to Boston, barged through the student's door, and furiously unleashed a Woody-style torrent of advice. In sum, he wasn't going to stand for a former player of his to be a quitter, or allow the boy to disappoint his family. Then he stomped out, permitting no response, and flew home (Brondfield, 1977, pp. 98-102). The young man stayed. As his players graduated, and more than 90 percent did, they took positions of responsibility in their communities and maintained strong loyalties to OSU and to the football program. Such loyalties were vital, especially to a man like Woody.

Testing the Will to Survive

A coach's life is filled with surprises, good and bad, but as Woody saw it, no coach could afford the luxury of self-pity. Rather, he must assume a positive attitude towards the job, no matter the disappointment. Never were these coaching attributes more severely tested than in the late 1950s and early 1960s when Woody's teams became the source of national scrutiny and campus politics.

The events that unfolded provide valuable lessons—success can not be taken for granted, and there's often more to a job than what is listed in the job description.

In 1955, Woody and his team were on a roll, having won back-to-back Big Ten Championships. His first 3 years at OSU had not been easy, but by 1955 he had gained the confidence of the campus, the alumni, and Buckeye fans in general. Then he granted an interview to a *Sports Illustrated* writer and casually mentioned in the interview that he sometimes helped a few of his players out with a little pocket money if they were especially in need. Like today, this was a violation of NCAA rules, although Woody hardly saw it as an evil and possibly wasn't even aware of the rule. After all, he had freely volunteered the information. As suggested by the article's title, "The Ohio State Story: Win or Else," Hayes came in for rough treatment. The violation clarification led to a Big Ten investigation, which further revealed that about 20 players held jobs where they were getting paid for doing little if any work. A one-year probation was imposed, and Buckeye euphoria over the 1955 team and their championship season plummeted.

From then on through the middle of the 1960s, there was a sustained and sharply focused attack on OSU's brand of big time football, "the machine" as it was called. A significant fraction of the OSU faculty and alumni were opposed to participation in the Rose Bowl and to the size and perceived importance of the OSU football program on the campus. Leading the assault was Jack Fullen, a prominent and active alum. As a helpful organizer for athletic fundraising, Fullen had been noted in the 1955 *Sports Illustrated* story. He also was editor of OSU's alumni magazine and wrote a weekly column in it. Soon after the *Sports Illustrated* story appeared, Fullen changed positions and began pounding away on his new pet theme: "The football tail is wagging the college dog" (Vare, 1974, p. 112). The attack Fullen led against the Rose Bowl was largely a matter of economics, and his facts and figures revealed that OSU made little more than expenses for the preparation and trip. The more fundamental issue, however, was values: football versus academics. Fullen called for more balance. As he saw it, OSU needed less money for football and more for students. He also went after Hayes personally.

Perhaps his most influential anti-Woody piece was published in 1961. During a game against Indiana, Woody had charged onto the field, in violation of the rules, to argue an interference call. Fullen reported the incident with a vivid essay (photos and all) of Hayes screaming, kicking, and flailing; he entitled the column, "The Gentle Art of Teaching."

That year, OSU had a record of 8-0-1, winning the Big Ten title and the number one national ranking in the UPI. As plans for the trip to Pasadena were being made throughout the world of Buckeyes, the OSU Faculty Council announced, after 90 minutes of bitter debate, that the team could not go to the Rose Bowl. The vote was 28 to 25 against participation.* Within hours, more than 10,000 students took to High Street and the campus rim, overturning cars and smashing windows. "No Rose Bowl, no classes" became their rallying cry, and the turmoil, violence, and distraction lasted three days and nights until the campus administration finally closed campus, threatening expulsion to any student caught demonstrating. No one perhaps was more embarrassed than the Athletic Director, Dick Larkin, who had told the Faculty Council just prior to their meeting that football was "nothing more than a popular extracurricular activity at Ohio State" (Vare, 1974, p. 117). The OSU riot preceded by more than two years the "free speech" riots led by Mario Savio at Berkeley in 1964. But the issues at OSU were not free speech, politics, and war; they were football, heroes, and dreams.

With their dreams shattered, it is a tribute to the character of Hayes and his players that they acted with positive restraint at the time. Woody was in Cleveland when word of the demonstrations reached him; he personally guaranteed the audience of alumni that none of his players would be involved. Events proved him right, and, with his prodding, some of his players took to the campus to help quell disturbances. Mike Ingram, the team's co-captain, was particularly influential, reminding the student mobs that if your team can live with this, so can you. Good conduct by the team, and strong student support were not enough, however, to reverse the council's decision. Hayes knew he had a long fight on his hands.

In January the 11 members of the Board of Directors of the Alumni Association, who had the power to fire Fullen as editor of the alumni magazine, instead gave him their unanimous vote of confidence. Meanwhile, Woody took to the road speaking to alumni

---

*Minnesota won the precarious honor of representing the Big Ten in the Rose Bowl that New Year's Day.

groups around the state and the nation. If he had been running a narrow-minded win-with-you-today, forget-you-tomorrow kind of football program, he might have been overwhelmed. Or if he had wallowed in self-pity, or lost sight of his purpose and goals, he surely would have lost the battle. Instead, he engaged his offensive thinking to win the war of values, pressing for grass roots support from ex-players, alumni, and friends. He reminded them that the Rose Bowl had been snatched from them too. Why should his exemplary players be denied the right to represent them, to show Buckeye pride, and to reach the highest levels of excellence they could?

In May of 1962, the war of values began leaning favorably to Woody's side. Four seats on the 11 member board were up for grabs at the annual alumni elections, and pro-Bowl (pro-Woody) forces won all four. New sentiments also found their way into the Faculty Council, and the administration helped matters by disallowing all expense paid trips to Pasadena for administrators and wives. After a year-long campaign, Woody finally prevailed, and the council's vote flip-flopped—36 to 20 in favor of participation whenever Buckeye teams were worthy.

It is easy to imagine most other men folding under such rejection. Does someone take up coaching to win and then be denied participation in the game of the year for the national championship? How easy it would be to turn bitter, scorn the university, and walk away to take a job elsewhere. Woody surely would have had no difficulty getting one. Instead, he rose to the attack and won the battle off the field with the help of many whom he had paid forward.

Bouncing Back and Looking Forward

When Hayes was fired over the phone in Miami 12 hours after trying to deck Charlie Bauman, sports scribes quickly took to pen and typewriter anticipating their final words on the great coach. Rarely has a man's fall from grace been so abrupt and, in Buckeye land, so clearly earth shattering. Columnist Kaye Kessler of the *Columbus Citizen-Journal* promptly (December 30, 1978) wrote "Great men should go out on shoulders and showered with praise, not with sorrow, head shaking, puzzlement and predicaments. . . . and Woody *was* a great man." His colleague Tom Pastorius (1978) began his coverage with "Woody is *gone.*" Another colleague, Tom Keyes (1978), wrote, "It is not my aim to make a martyr of Hayes, but there is enough compassion in me to ask a question that seems pertinent at this time: Are the great fans of Ohio going to ignore all the good things Woody Hayes did here and remember him only as a man who was shot down without a hearing for his *final*, unpardonable transgression?" "Was," "gone," "final"—words that left no doubt that those who had studied and written about him thought he was finished. Their columns might as well have appeared amidst the obituaries.

Other men might have wallowed in self-righteous pity, felt bitter, and taken to living in the past, but not Woody. Here again he lived out his philosophy, true to his own words: " 'The lesson football teaches is that when you get knocked down you get up and move again' " (Hornung, 1982, p. 9). So often had he said this to his players, it became virtually a cliché. He was determined to show that he could take a punch as well as throw one.

A helpful boost to Woody's spirits was promptly provided by his former players, who visited him sometimes five to six in number per day. When a group of them organized a banquet in his honor, more than 450 attended. With money raised through the banquet, his players reconstructed a 100-year-old cabin on a wooded hill in Noble County where he could go to write and think. They knew he wasn't about to quit, not at age 66. He would just change and move on with forward thinking in a new direction.

Woody Hayes after retirement from coaching.

As he later told his close friend, columnist Paul Hornung of the *Columbus Dispatch,* " 'I don't take this thing as seriously as most people; to hell with it. I'm not going to let anything get in my way. I don't live in the past' " (1982, p. 9).*

Woody waited about three whole weeks after "the incident" before making his first public appearance. To most people's astonishment, he made good on his commitment to speak at the annual meeting of the Columbus Area Chamber of Commerce. This routinely dull event was perhaps never so lively. Hayes's typical blockbuster speech, full of history, philosophy, and advice, was broadcast live on radio before a capacity audience and was printed verbatim in the article "Ousted Hayes Still Heaps Praise at OSU" (*Columbus Dispatch*). He rendered a carefully worded note of regret for his misdeed, but no apology. A week later, again to most people's surprise, he attended the Touchdown Club's annual dinner and presented Penn State's Joe Paterno with the Woody Hayes Trophy for the year's outstanding college coach. The audience welcomed Hayes to the stage with a standing ovation.

Aside from meeting these commitments and accepting his replacement's adamant request to attend a 1979 training table dinner for the players, Woody stayed away from the team and divorced himself from the OSU football scene. Hayes and the new coach, Earle Bruce, shared mutual respect and were friends, for Bruce had worked as Woody's assistant for six years. But Woody saw it this way: " 'Earle is the Ohio State football coach . . . it's his show now. I'm not going to horn in in any way' " (Hornung, 1982, p. 10). Woody stayed committed, but he watched the games privately on TV at home.

Denied the football field, Woody sought other ways of paying forward, mainly through giving speeches. As a gifted speaker, he took pride in speaking to many different groups, sometimes for a hefty fee, but more often for free. He viewed himself as a pushover for groups without money, and his most frequent speeches were for schools trying to keep their athletic programs going after the board of education had cut athletics funds.

There is no denying that aging changes a man, and Woody's attitude about his past slowly changed too. Where he had once forbade people telling stories about some of the things he had done

---

*As reported in the *Sacramento Bee* on May 21, 1991, Woody Hayes was later known to have said, "They give you a Cadillac one year, and the next year they give you the gas to get out of town."

for them, he began allowing it. Wider audiences learned of the stories about his regular visits to hospitals to read to sick kids, about the badgering he gave his players and others to study and graduate from school, and about the speeches he gave freely to groups because he liked their values. Woody stayed on a course of exemplary behavior.

By 1982, Woody had reached a new pinnacle of admiration and distinction, and the image of Hayes the villain had dimmed. Woody the softie and the philosopher emerged, and the accolades and honors began pouring in. Shortly after his keynote speech at Harvard commemorating Emerson, he was honored in Columbus at a roast that raised more than $40,000 to help underprivileged young athletes. About the same time a bronze bust of Hayes was placed at the Children's Hospital memorializing him for his services to hospitalized children. He was also awarded the Ohio State Distinguished Service Award, and the university had the main street passing by the OSU sports complex renamed Woody Hayes Drive. The presentations of the award and the street naming came from none other than OSU President Edward Jennings, with the unanimous approval of the school's Board of Trustees. In short, it took little more than three years after he was fired in disgrace for the same institution to pay him some of its highest honors. Early in 1986, OSU went even further; Professor W.W. Hayes received the following official letter, dated January 31, 1986, from Edward H. Jennings, President of Ohio State University:

> In conversations about excellence at the Ohio State University, your name is invariably mentioned. . . . The achievements and honors that have brought you national recognition and respect over the years also have brought great credit to Ohio State. Your long record of outstanding accomplishment and your well-known dedication to the academic enterprise are symbolic of this university.

> For these reasons, you have been chosen to receive an Honorary Doctorate Degree to be conferred upon you at the Winter Commencement exercises on Friday, March 21, 1986.

> It is with special pleasure that I also invite you to honor the university community by delivering the Commencement address. . . .*

---

*I am grateful to John Mount, a close colleague and friend of Woody's at Ohio State University, for supplying this statement to me.

When Woody died, Archie Griffin*, two time Heisman Trophy winner, said, " 'It was like a bomb. It feels like my father had passed away. He was like a father to us players' " (Strode, 1987, p. 1-A). Two weeks after Archie's dad died, Archie and I chatted on the phone reflectively (February 13, 1991). He said, "Yes, Woody's death came to mind. It was like I had two fathers; they were always there to help me."

Few people experience such public warmth and affection. In William Shakespeare's immortal words, "The evil that men do lives after them. The good is oft interred with their bones. So let it be with Caesar." For Caesar, perhaps it was, but not for Woody. His deeds, good and bad, glow still in our memory and remind us that imperfect men can be mighty examples of strength, wisdom, and character.

W.W. "Woody" Hayes Coaching Facts

- Wayne Woodrow "Woody" Hayes served 28 years as head football coach at The Ohio State University. Only Amos Alonzo Stagg, 41 years at Chicago, and Bob Zuppke, at Illinois for 29 years, coached longer in the Big Ten.

- Under Hayes, Ohio State football achieved a degree of excellence unmatched in the university's rich athletic history. Winning seasons and conference championships were a familiar part of the Buckeye football scene under Hayes.

- With 238 wins, Hayes ranks fourth among all major college coaches in terms of victories. Only Paul "Bear" Bryant, Glenn Pop Warner, and Amos Alonzo Stagg managed more wins than Hayes.

- Hayes's record at Ohio State was a remarkable 205 wins, 61 losses, and 10 ties, a winning percentage of .760. His Big Ten record was 152-37-7. While he coached at Ohio State, the Buckeyes led the nation in attendance per home game 21 times in 28 years and finished a close second the other seven seasons.

- Numerous honors were won by Coach Hayes and by his Ohio State teams. He was named "College Coach of the Year" in 1957

---

*Archie Griffin is presently the assistant athletic Director at OSU and a prominent citizen in Ohio.

and 1975, and was runnerup for this honor on two other occasions. He coached three Heisman Award winners and 56 first team All-Americans. He was a past president of the National Football Coaches' Association.

- His Ohio State teams won three national championships; 13 Big Ten championships; won a record 17 straight Big Ten victories two different times (1954-56 and 1967-69); and played in 11 bowl games, eight Rose Bowls, one Orange Bowl, one Sugar Bowl and one Gator Bowl. Ohio State is the only eastern team in the history of the Rose Bowl to make four consecutive appearances.

- Hayes was born February 14, 1913, in Clifton, Ohio, although he called Newcomerstown his home. He was a 1935 graduate of Denison University, where he majored in English and history. He played tackle three years and was an outfielder in baseball. He held an M.A. degree from Ohio State in education administration.

- His entire coaching career was within the state of Ohio. His first coaching job was in 1935 as an assistant at Mingo Junction. His first head coaching job came in 1938 at New Philadelphia High, where in three seasons, his teams won 19, lost 10, and tied 1.

- A five-year stint in the Navy interrupted his coaching career but made a great impact upon his life.

- After his discharge, Denison University, his alma mater, gave him his first opportunity to be a head coach in college. The year was 1946. Three years at Denison and two at Miami set the stage for his 1951 debut at Ohio State.

Woody Hayes's Head Coaching Record

Year	Team	Won	Lost	Tied	Percent	Points	Opponent's points
1946	Denison	2	6	0	.250	89	136
1947#	Denison	9	0	0	1.000	274	54
1948#	Denison	8	0	0	1.000	277	54
3 year totals		19	6	0	.760	640	243
1949	Miami	5	4	0	.556	251	163
1950#	Miami	9	1	0	.900	356	100
2 year totals		14	5	0	.737	607	263
1951	Ohio State	4	3	2	.556	109	104
1952	Ohio State	6	3	0	.667	197	119
1953	Ohio State	6	3	0	.667	182	164
1954#+	Ohio State	10	0	0	1.000	249	75
1955#	Ohio State	7	2	0	.778	201	97
1956	Ohio State	6	3	0	.667	160	81
1957#+	Ohio State	9	1	0	.900	267	92
1958	Ohio State	6	1	2	.778	182	132
1959	Ohio State	3	5	1	.389	83	114
1960	Ohio State	7	2	0	.778	209	90
1961#	Ohio State	8	0	1	.944	221	83
1962	Ohio State	6	3	0	.667	205	98
1963	Ohio State	5	3	1	.611	110	102
1964	Ohio State	7	2	0	.778	146	76
1965	Ohio State	7	2	0	.778	156	118
1966	Ohio State	4	5	0	.444	108	123
1967	Ohio State	6	3	0	.667	145	120
1968#+	Ohio State	10	0	0	1.000	323	150
1969#	Ohio State	8	1	0	.889	383	93
1970#+	Ohio State	9	1	0	.900	290	120
1971	Ohio State	6	4	0	.600	224	120
1972#+	Ohio State	9	2	0	.818	280	171
1973#+	Ohio State	10	0	1	.954	413	64
1974#+	Ohio State	10	2	0	.883	437	129
1975#+	Ohio State	11	1	0	.916	384	102
1976#*	Ohio State	9	2	1	.791	305	149

(Cont.)

Woody Hayes's Head Coaching Record (Continued)

Year	Team	Won	Lost	Tied	Percent	Points	Opponent's points
1977#%	Ohio State	9	3	0	.750	343	120
1978 &	Ohio State	7	4	1	.625	339	216
28 year totals		205	61	10	.760	6,651	3,222
33 year totals		238	72	10	.759	7,898	3,324

Conference Champion
+ Rose Bowl
* Orange Bowl
% Sugar Bowl
& Gator Bowl

Chapter 3

John Wooden:
From Basics to Baskets

Ten Titles in Twelve Years

In 1964, the Beatles invaded America, Martin Luther King won the Noble Peace Prize, North Vietnamese patrol boats attacked U.S. ships in the Gulf of Tonkin, Mario Savio sparked the Free Speech Movement at Berkeley, and John Wooden's Bruins won UCLA's first NCAA basketball championship.

In 1965, President Lyndon Baines Johnson announced his vision of a "Great Society," the U.S. launched air strikes in North Vietnam and unleashed ground forces in South Vietnam, Cassius Clay

John Wooden at a game with his game program, an inseparable trademark, giving an instruction to the players.

renamed himself Muhammad Ali then whipped Sonny Liston for a second time to retain the Heavyweight title, and race riots raged in Watts for five days. Once again, Wooden's Bruins won the NCAA title.

In 1973, the U.S. agreed in Paris to stop fighting in Vietnam, Vice President Spiro Agnew resigned from office, the televised Watergate investigation provided daily intrigue to a cynical dispirited world, and Bill Walton, one of the year's tallest cynics, led the Bruins to their seventh straight NCAA title.

In 1975, Watergate criminals John Mitchell, H.R. Haldeman, and John Ehrlichman headed for jail, Nixon endured his suffering as a free man thanks to President Ford's pardon, Saigon surrendered to the Communists who also captured Cambodia, and Britain's Conservative Party elected its first woman leader. That same year John Wooden announced his retirement shortly before coaching UCLA to its tenth NCAA basketball championship.

When this episodic twelve-year period of history began, Bob Dylan wailed his hit song "Times They Are A-Changing," but in this era of drugs, dropouts, protests, war, resignations, and assassinations—one man changed little. John Wooden bent with the times, but he never broke from his fundamental values and ways.

Time and Place

Imagine anyone, at any time, forecasting a similar reign of dominance in college basketball; it's laughable. Even five championships in nearly as many years is beyond comprehension. Furthermore, Wooden's unmatchable reign* seems in retrospect all the more incomprehensible because of the era and the place, for few states could rival California as a frontrunner in the turmoil of those times. While Berkeley had student activist Mario Savio and others, UCLA had teacher activist Angela Davis and others. Watts isn't far from Westwood, and generally speaking, to campus youth in the 60s and early 70s, defiance was the only conformity that was "in."

---

*It could have been longer. In 1962, UCLA lost in a final four game by only two points to Cincinnati who went on to win the championship; in 1966 the Freshman Rule, now no longer applicable, kept Lew Alcindor (Kareem Abdul-Jabbar) from playing on the varsity team.

How could anyone have won year after year in Los Angeles in the 1960s and 1970s? Somewhere in the Midwest, perhaps, or elsewhere where life evolved instead of convulsed, but John Wooden not only did the impossible—10 NCAA wins in 12 years—but he did it in the worst of times in a hot spot of trouble. How this was accomplished has puzzled many coaches and sports enthusiasts; yet answers defy us and probably always will. It matters not. The struggle to find an explanation is more useful than any final answer. The striving to learn Wooden's contributions to his teams and others compels us not from any desire for another string of wins, but rather for a broader sense of what makes people better.

To begin, it is important to remember that it was the coaching philosophy of a Midwesterner, a man ingrained with old-fashioned salt of the earth ideals and values that pulled off this unbelievable string of victories. A farm boy product of the Great Depression, his credo was homespun and simple: hard purposeful work, pride, and selflessness. Wooden was not a man of his time, the 1960s and 1970s, nor even of this century according to his biographers Chapin and Prugh (1973).

> His major victories, as a coach, have come in his later years, in the twentieth century. But he might be more at home in the nineteenth century, running a white, frame, one-room school as principal and teacher, and maybe serving one night a week as unpaid village mayor.

> He has existed and bent in the world of ban the bombs, the bras, and the bullshit, but if you had to place him it would be in a time capsule of a different world—horse-drawn buggies, gas lamps, and Sunday afternoon picnics, after church, down on the banks of the Wabash. Occasionally, he'd crane his neck and look out into the next century but then he'd withdraw into the time capsule again. (p. 318)*

To elaborate on the obvious, John Wooden wasn't glitzy, and, as a displaced Hoosier from Indiana, he seemed out of place in Westwood, California. As Jim Murray, a *Los Angeles Times* correspondent, described him, " 'He's so square; he's divisible by four' "

---

*From *The Wizard of Westwood* by Dwight Chapin and Jethro Prugh. Copyright © 1973 by Dwight Chapin and Jethro Prugh. Reprinted by permission of Houghton Mifflin Company.

(Chapin & Prugh, 1973, p. 320). During a wide-ranging conversation at his home in 1987, I asked Coach Wooden if there were some things he was ashamed of or wished he hadn't done. (We'd been speaking about morals.) He replied, "I smoked cigarettes for awhile when I was a young man. Picked it up early. So there's one, and I'm embarrassed to tell you that on a few occasions I've used profanity." That was it, and I didn't reply.

For Wooden, dishonesty was unthinkable, as was flamboyance. There can be no doubt that Wooden won without gimmicks or tricks. As he was prone to say, "If you keep too busy learning the tricks of the trade, you may never learn the trade" (1972, p. 110). The media had much to write about Wooden, but as many observers noted, his daily life and personal character seemed too dull to write about. It's probably fair to say that the press was essentially neutral on him; it hardly gave him a boost beyond reporting the facts of his wins. But no matter—he didn't need the media's help. He had his own formula for success.

Formula for Success

Success, that great illusion, begs for definition, and few people can claim it with the assurance of John Wooden. His own conscious quest for understanding success began as a high school boy in Martinsville, Indiana when one of his teachers gave his class an assignment to define it: Is there a formula to insure success? For years and years that question returned to taunt Wooden. As Wooden explained in his videotape *Pyramid of Success* (1984), "Long ago I wasn't satisfied with what was generally considered to be success, which was the accumulation of material possessions or the attainment of a position of power or prestige. I don't think those things necessarily indicate success, but they might. So after a lot of thinking I came up with my own definition." It was as a teacher in South Bend that he first began to develop a method to help his students understand how to judge success. Additional years and hundreds of hours of work would pass before he finished his own definition of success. He constructed his formula as a pyramid, like the most durable of monuments built by man. Placing his definition of success at the top, he called it his "Pyramid of Success." As he tells it, "It may be the only truly original thing I ever did."*

---

*From *The Pyramid of Success*, distributed by the UCLA Sport Information Office.

Wooden's pyramid is a worthy foundation for anyone building their own formula or definition, for in explaining it Wooden admonishes everyone that *success is a very personal matter*. Only you can judge success for yourself. In work, or play, or any activity, only you know whether or not you gave it your best. No one else can know for sure if you took the easy way out, cut corners, shirked, or freeloaded on the efforts of others to accomplish something. Even Wooden acknowledges that he can look back with regret on what seemed to others to be success. Who can't?

The structural foundation to Wooden's pyramid is the key to success. As shown in Figure 1, the cornerstones are *industriousness* and *enthusiasm*. To convey the role industriousness plays, especially in athletic success, Wooden is fond of reciting these words from Grantland Rice's, "How to Be a Champion."

> "You wonder how they do it and you
> look to see the knack,
> You watch the foot in action, or the
> shoulder, or the back,
> But when you spot the answer where
> the higher glamours lurk,
> You'll find in moving higher up the
> laurel covered spire,
> That the most of it is practice and the
> rest of it is work."
> (Wooden, 1972, pp. 88-89)

The other cornerstone, enthusiasm, is a matter of the heart; we must enjoy our work and stimulate others. Completing the base between the cornerstones are the blocks *friendship, cooperation,* and *loyalty*. When presenting and discussing his pyramid with his players, Wooden emphasized both the similarity of these interior base blocks and the importance of a united effort to lock in the cornerstones. In other words, great accomplishments and best efforts rest on a base of joyous hard work that sustains enthusiasm and integrates individual skills and efforts in an atmosphere of cooperation, personal regard, and commitment.

Resting above the base blocks on the ends are the key blocks of *self-control* and *intentness*. The loss of self-control can cause an immediate failure, and no one can function in top form mentally and physically unless emotions are in control. Indeed, Wooden had

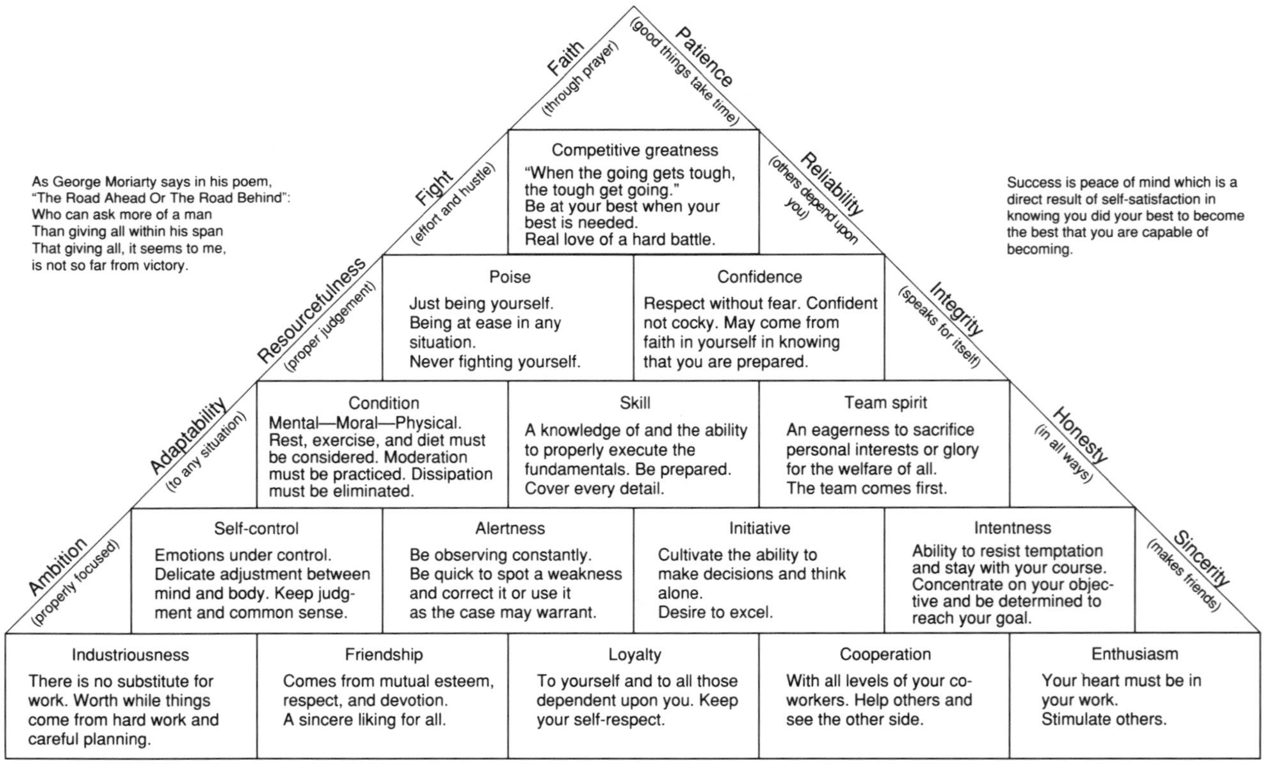
As George Moriarty says in his poem,
"The Road Ahead Or The Road Behind":
Who can ask more of a man
Than giving all within his span
That giving all, it seems to me,
is not so far from victory.
Success is peace of mind which is a direct result of self-satisfaction in knowing you did your best to become the best that you are capable of becoming.
Faith (through prayer)
Patience (good things take time)
Fight (effort and hustle)
Reliability (others depend upon you)
Resourcefulness (proper judgement)
Integrity (speaks for itself)
Adaptability (to any situation)
Honesty (in all ways)
Ambition (properly focused)
Sincerity (makes friends)
Competitive greatness
"When the going gets tough, the tough get going."
Be at your best when your best is needed.
Real love of a hard battle.
Poise
Just being yourself.
Being at ease in any situation.
Never fighting yourself.
Confidence
Respect without fear. Confident not cocky. May come from faith in yourself in knowing that you are prepared.
Condition
Mental—Moral—Physical.
Rest, exercise, and diet must be considered. Moderation must be practiced. Dissipation must be eliminated.
Skill
A knowledge of and the ability to properly execute the fundamentals. Be prepared.
Cover every detail.
Team spirit
An eagerness to sacrifice personal interests or glory for the welfare of all.
The team comes first.
Self-control
Emotions under control.
Delicate adjustment between mind and body. Keep judg-ment and common sense.
Alertness
Be observing constantly.
Be quick to spot a weakness and correct it or use it as the case may warrant.
Initiative
Cultivate the ability to make decisions and think alone.
Desire to excel.
Intentness
Ability to resist temptation and stay with your course.
Concentrate on your objec-tive and be determined to reach your goal.
Industriousness
There is no substitute for work. Worth while things come from hard work and careful planning.
Friendship
Comes from mutual esteem, respect, and devotion.
A sincere liking for all.
Loyalty
To yourself and to all those dependent upon you. Keep your self-respect.
Cooperation
With all levels of your co-workers. Help others and see the other side.
Enthusiasm
Your heart must be in your work.
Stimulate others.

Figure 1 John Wooden's pyramid of success. Coach Wooden often said this may be the only truly original thing that he has done. It was originated and developed in the late 1930s in an effort for his own self-improvement as a high school teacher and coach. He feels that adherence to the blocks of the pyramid encourages individuals to become the best they are capable of becoming, regardless of how they may be judged by others. *Note.* Reprinted by permission of John Wooden.

a firm policy to never charge up his team on an emotional level with pep talks and rah-rah inspiration. He wanted his players calm. Constant steady progress is preferable, according to Wooden, to hitting a number of peaks. Valleys follow peaks as disappointment follows joy. He wanted his players to recognize clearly the basis of good things and avoid being captured by self-pity when misfortunes arose. The object of intentness is to avoid distractions and resist temptations. What the distractions consist of depends on the goal; intentness must be focused on a selected goal.

Alertness and *initiative* cement the second tier together and to the base. Being constantly alert and seeking new ways to improve are essential to progress—individual progress and team progress. Initiative is imperative for acting on the opportunity once recognized. In sports competition, an athlete must be alert to see an opponent's mistakes or weaknesses and must have the strength of character to capitalize on them. Similarly, in business, competitors must be alert for new opportunities and have the courage to make decisions to take advantage of them.

In the center—the heart—of Wooden's vision of success are *condition, skill,* and *team spirit.* Of course, in thinking about condition it is natural to immediately relate it to physical condition. Wooden (1972), however, argues that

> you cannot attain and maintain physical condition unless you are morally and mentally conditioned. . . . I tell my players that our team condition depends on two factors—how hard they work on the floor during practice and how well they behave between practices. You can neither attain nor maintain proper condition without working at both. (pp. 89-90)

Skill also requires elaboration, for it is more than the knowledge and proper execution of fundamentals. Skills must be applied, and in sports competition at least, they must be applied quickly and at exactly the right moment. These reactions to events or opportunities should be instinctive. Wooden told me he used to tell his players, "Act quickly but don't hurry." Conditioning the instincts is critical to accomplish this. As he often said, "Failure to prepare is preparing to fail" (Capouya, 1986, p. 140).

As will be further emphasized later, team spirit and selflessness were as central to Wooden's game plan as they are to his pyramid of success. Wooden (1972) defined team spirit and explained its importance as follows:

This is an eagerness to sacrifice personal glory for the welfare of the group as a whole. It's togetherness and consideration for others. If players are not considerate of one another, there is no way we can have the proper team play that is needed. It is not necessary for everyone to particularly like each other to play well together, but they must respect each other and subordinate selfishness to the welfare of the team. The team must come first. (p. 90)

The blocks *poise, confidence,* and *competitive greatness* lie just below Wooden's pinnacle where he defines success. For Wooden, poise and confidence extend from and are fundamentally determined by condition, skill, and team spirit. To be in condition, to have finely honed skills, and to possess the proper team spirit are to be prepared. Being prepared and knowing oneself to be prepared assure poise and confidence.

As these blocks fall into place competitive greatness naturally results and permits heroic acts of achievement that realize one's full potential. Wooden (1972) admonishes us that "Every block is built upon the other. One will not succeed without the other, and when all are in place, you are on the road toward success. If one crumbles, it may lead to the breakdown of all" (p. 90). To further illustrate the elements of competitive greatness, Wooden (1972) again turns to the writings of Grantland Rice, namely to his poem, "The Great Competitor":

> "Beyond the winning and the goal, be-
> yond the glory and the flame,
> He feels the flame within his soul, born
> of the spirit of the game,
> And where the barriers may wait, built
> up by the opposing Gods,
> He finds a thrill in bucking fate and
> riding down the endless odds.
> Where others lag behind or tire and break
> beneath the handicap,
> He finds a new and deeper thrill to take
> him on the uphill spin.
> Because the test is greater still, and some-
> thing he can revel in."
> (pp. 90-91)

John Wooden, a man with peace of mind.

The mortar on the sides providing cohesion to the blocks are other components of wisdom. Working up the pyramid from the bottom right side are the keys to making friends: *sincerity, honesty, integrity, reliability.* From bottom left upwards are *ambition, adaptability, resourcefulness,* and *fight. Faith* and *patience* cement the top for Wooden's definition of success: "Success is peace of mind which is a direct result of self-satisfaction in knowing you did your best to become the best you are capable of becoming."

Lessons on Life

When Wooden held his traditional team meeting early each season, he handed out the rules, regulations, practice and game schedules—and his pyramid flyer. The flyer conveyed no magical formula for scoring points; its purpose was to chart a thought process, a special kind of motivation. One of the reasons Wooden had agreed in 1948 to come to UCLA from Indiana State was to have the freedom to teach this philosophy. He wanted to teach ideas, not just skills. He wanted inner motivation from his athletes. The main focus was to be on the self not on the opponents, and

Wooden never once scouted opposing teams. His own teams played with confidence about their ability—the peace of mind of knowing they were at their best and were prepared to do their best as a team. Wooden tried to keep his teams from feeling outside pressures, and psychologically they benefited from that.

Personal definitions of success, as Wooden notes, will and should vary. What Wooden provided his players, and others he has influenced, was a foundation and a perspective on which to build a successful life. He challenged them to individually improve on the structure. He did not aim at final answers, but provided a promising direction for all to pursue—a direction in life as well as in basketball. A clean pathway through life was his primary gift to his players and was the key to his own coaching success.

We can only guess abut the varying first reactions of most of his players, many with anxious minds to get on with the workouts, when Wooden set them down for a review and explanation of his pyramid of success. Much of his lecturing, of course, didn't penetrate at first, but eventually a lot of it did. Wooden told me that Kareem Abdul-Jabbar only started to study the pyramid and analyze it for himself in his junior year. Kareem partially collaborated this observation:

> "The first time I saw it, I didn't pay any attention to it. I think maybe my junior or senior year I started to look at it a little more closely, but I still never really paid much attention to it. And then somebody tried to tell me that he was a mason, and [laughing] I asked him about that, and he said no he wasn't a mason, that was just something he had devised that he thought worked. I think I really paid the closest attention to it my first year or two in the pros when I was getting into more adult situations, and I saw how it transcended basketball." (Wooden, 1984)

According to Wooden, Kareem improved in participation, and the team as a whole worked together better during Abdul-Jabbar's junior and senior years than at any other time before or after. Walt Hazzard also told of his reaction to Wooden's pyramid:

> "I know the very first day of practice he passed out the Pyramid of Success to all the team and reviewed it. And he always reminded us of those things as the year went on. He had a lot of wisdom, a lot of vision, in terms of understanding what it

took to make a group of young men work together toward one goal, and he did it better than anyone who's ever done it in the history of collegiate basketball." (Wooden, 1984)

Sidney Wicks, one of the other great stars from UCLA, has often lectured at summer basketball camps and the like. In his talks he refers to the pyramid, saying, " 'You suddenly realize that all those things Coach Wooden harps on all the time are true' " (Wooden, 1972, p. 93).

Although a number of people over the years have encouraged Wooden to copyright and sell the pyramid, he has steadfastly refused. His preference has been to use it as it was intended: as a teaching tool to give direction to people on the pathway to a successful life. Money, power, and fame are to Wooden mere symptoms of success. Real success is in our own mind not in the hand, bank account, or in the minds of others.

Teaching Methods

John Wooden lived, coached, and won by his credo: hard purposeful work, pride, and selflessness. He lived and taught these basic virtues like few others in his day. And few could match his skills as a teacher. So thorough was his lesson plan that some of his first moments with freshmen were spent teaching them how to properly put on their sweat socks. As Wooden (1972) put it, "No basketball player is better than his feet. If they hurt, if his shoes don't fit, or if he has blisters, he can't play the game. It is amazing how few players know how to put on a pair of socks properly. I don't want blisters, so each year I give in minute detail a step-by-step demonstration as to precisely how I want them to put on their socks—every time" (p. 106). As these words convey, Wooden was convinced that every detail was important and that success usually accompanied such attention to minor details.

In John Wooden's last season (1974-1975) as coach at UCLA, Roland G. Tharp and Ronald Gallimore acted on a hunch they had nurtured for several years. Recognizing that Wooden had coached all kinds of players year after year, and had taught them how to be champions, they reasoned that his educational techniques must have been superior. After all, 10 NCAA championships in 12 years had to result from either luck, superior recruiting talents, superior specialized knowledge about how to play to win, superior technique in teaching and coaching effectively, or some combination thereof. Luck as an answer was blatantly doubtful, for Wooden's career showed too much consistency. Clearly talent galore came to UCLA, but Wooden won with small players as well as big ones, and Wooden himself confessed that he was more reactive in recruiting than proactive. For example, it was Lew Alcindor's (Kareem Abdul-Jabbar) parents, not Wooden, who initiated the great star's contact with UCLA, and most of Wooden's meetings with recruits were established through his assistants. Wooden made no more than a dozen recruiting trips in his entire career. As a recruiter, he was essentially passive. And, though no one would question his vast knowledge of the game, his style of play and patterns of offense and defense were subject to imitation. Moreover, as mentioned earlier, he never once scouted an opposing team. Why couldn't other coaches, with equal luck, recruiting ability, and play-by-play know-how match Wooden's record? Tharp and Gallimore believed his teaching ability was the reason.

Tharp and Gallimore, as psychologists and academicians, analyzed Wooden's teaching methods for the purpose of conveying them to other educators. It is doubtful that any classroom educator has ever been so closely and scientifically scrutinized for teaching effectiveness. The results of their observations and analysis were published in the January 1976 issue of *Psychology Today*.

Tharp and Gallimore used categories for observation that they had derived from years of clinical research on educational methods: reinforcement, punishment, instruction, and modeling. With this standard observation-category system, they observed Wooden in eight practices over several weeks and developed a systematic recording system that could be clearly tabulated for use by others. Those tabulations are shown in Table 3.1 and include two categories the researchers had not thought of or witnessed until seeing Wooden at work. These two "Wooden Categories" are (1) scold/reinstruction—basically criticism followed instantly by correction, and (2) "hustle"—verbal cues directing the players. After determining these categories, they collected data from 15 sessions. They placed themselves in the front row of Pauley Pavilion—close enough to see and hear 93 percent of Wooden's exchanges with the players.

Although Wooden's teaching and coaching transcended the formal practices, he notes in his autobiography (1972) "My talks with

Table 3.1
John Wooden at Work: How He Talks to His Team

Code	Category	Description	Percent of total communications
I	Instruction	Verbal statements about what to do, or how to do it	50.3
H	Hustles	Verbal statements to activate or intensify previously instructed behavior	12.7
M+	Modeling-positive	A demonstration of how to perform	2.8
M−	Modeling-negative	A demonstration of how not to perform	1.6
V+	Praises	Verbal compliments, encouragements	6.9
V−	Scolds	Verbal statements of displeasure	6.6
NV+	Nonverbal reward	Nonverbal compliments or encouragements (smiles, pats, jokes)	1.2
NV−	Nonverbal punishment	This infrequent category included only scowls, gestures of despair, and temporary removal of a player from scrimmage, usually to shoot free throws by himself	Trace
W	Scold/reinstruction	A combination category: a single verbal behavior which refers to a specific act, contains a clear scold, and reasserts a previously instructed behavior; e.g., "How many times do I have to tell you to follow through with your head when shooting?"	8.0
O	Other	Any behavior not falling into the above categories	2.4
X	Uncodable	The behavior could not be clearly heard or seen	6.6

Note. From Tharp and Gallimore (1976). Reprinted by permission.

the players usually take place right on the floor during practice. I'm not a believer in meetings or so called chalk talks or blackboard drills" (p. 107). Table 3.1, therefore, reflects Wooden the teacher. It summarizes 30 hours of observation by Tharp and Gallimore and classifies 2,326 separate observations. The following information from their article in *Psychology Today* further elaborates on Table 3.1:

• After the warm-up, practice begins with conditioning drills. He [Wooden] continually shouts instructions (first category in the table) on the fundamentals of movement, dribbling and defense. Instructions constitute half (50.3 percent) of his total teaching acts, and even this statistic does not adequately reflect the heavy freight of information Wooden communicates.

• After conditioning drills comes fast-break practice. During this and similar drills, hustles occur most often (12.7 percent of all acts). A hustle, defined as verbal statements to activate or intensify previously instructed behavior, is in reality the coach shouting, "Drive! Drive! Harder! Hustle! Hustle!" In addition to their function as cues, hustles may serve some players as scolds and others as positive reinforcement.

• But between the whistles that start and end practice, he is a dead-serious teacher whose reproofs can be so withering that observing psychologists shrink in their seats. Example: "No, No, No. Some of you are just standing around watching. Play your man tight before he gets the ball. Goodness gracious sakes, use the head the good Lord gave you.

• The aspect of Wooden's teaching with the greatest theoretical value is his unexpected mix of social reinforcement and punishment. In direct contrast to the techniques advocated by many behavior modifiers, praise is a minor feature of Wooden's teaching methods. . . . Wooden scolds twice as much as he rewards.

• In no sense is Wooden mean or punitive. He almost always ends practice with a light touch, a joke, an affectionate pat on the back for players on the tired trek to the locker room. He never uses physical punishment such as lap-running. He prefers to keep practice a desirable activity.

• Repetition is a canon in Wooden's learning theory. "I believe" he says, "in learning by repetition to the point where everything becomes automatic . . . the best teacher is repetition, day after day, throughout the season."

- Perhaps the example of greatest artistry is his use of modeling. His demonstrations are rarely longer than five seconds, but they are of such clarity as to leave an image in memory much like a textbook sketch.

- We can state that at least 75 percent of Wooden's teaching acts carry information. This information density is clearly a significant feature of his success. When he coaches, Wooden wastes few words on generalities.

Years after the Tharp and Gallimore study, a *Sports Illustrated* article (Wolff, 1989) would also emphasize Wooden's teaching methods:

> Wooden taught basketball according to the simplest pedagogical principles. He used what he calls the whole-part method. Show the whole and then break it down, "just like parsing a sentence," he says, "or solving a math problem." He followed his four laws of learning: explanation, demonstration, correction and repetition. For 16 years there was talk of a new gym, and when UCLA finally opened Pauley Pavilion in 1965, Wooden made sure he didn't get just an arena, but a classroom with bleachers that roll back. (p. 100)

Wooden's teaching methods, important in their own right, provide only a glimmer of the subject that so vitally affected his student athletes. What he taught most emphatically were human values and the positive instincts for the game that he had learned and developed himself as a young player in Indiana. He taught ideas and concepts as well as skills. His own coach at Purdue, "Piggy" Lambert, insisted on team play and was a master of conditioning and game fundamentals. Playing as a team was a passion for Lambert, and selflessness, according to Lambert, was Wooden's finest virtue. It was primarily his selfless team playing that propelled Wooden into the Basketball Hall of Fame as a player. He remains the only man to receive this honor both as a player and as a coach, and selflessness became a cornerstone of the Wooden game plan.

Selflessness and Team Unity

In 1989 Tom Peters, co-author of *In Search of Excellence*, chose Robert Whiting's, *You Gotta Have Wa* for the book of the year on Japanese affairs. It was a surprising selection for Peters, because rather than discussing management and organization, the book's subject is baseball, Japanese baseball. Whereas many Americans believe that good baseball players are born and not made, the Japanese hold the opposite view. According to Whiting, the key steps to success in Japanese baseball are work, will, team spirit and unity (*wa*), and the pursuit of perfection ("One thousand days to learn, ten thousand days to refine" ["Lessons From Japan's Athletes," 1989, p. G-2]). One might suspect from this that Wooden's credo is common knowledge, at least in Japan.

To many Americans, however, the so-called virtues of Japanese methods seem senseless, and in some cases, even silly. Individuality is cherished in America even in sports. But one doesn't have to go to extremes—like the Tokyo Giants, for example, who have a rule prohibiting private conversations between players on the field, or like the manager of the Hanshin Tigers who insists that his players remove their caps and bow when he and the coaching staff walk onto the field—to gain insight into the profitable direction of change encouraged by the contrast of our cultures.

Like Japanese coaches, Wooden sought players that naturally exuded the virtues of work, will, and *wa*, and he hammered on individuality when it shortchanged *wa*. That took a lot of hammering, for it's probably fair to say that Wooden's pipeline of freshmen talent, like that of most coaches, was filled with boys who came to college with dreams of their own stardom. After all, most of them were high school stars of varying degrees of brilliance. Wooden's job was to cluster them into even greater illumination. At this task, the no-nonsense Wooden was profoundly effective. As Tharp and Gallimore note in their report on Wooden's teaching, with Wooden there was

> No Room for Grandstanders. Some players who were individual stars in high school are eager, when they get to UCLA, to dramatize their skill by fancy ball handling, jazzy dribbling, and behind-the-back or blind passing. They quickly learn that showboating is forbidden. Concentration on fundamentals is the name of the Wooden game, and on his superbly drilled teams there's no room for the grandstanding ego. (p. 76)

As Wooden told his players, "When you come to practice, you cease to exist as an individual. You're part of a team ("Wooden's Way," 1972).

To forge these unselfish traits in his players, Wooden exemplified and preached the virtues of selfless behavior and team unity. To do this he used reminders like "The true athlete should have character, not be a character" (1972, p. 49), or another of his favorites, "It is amazing how much can be accomplished if no one cares who gets the credit" (p. 105).* Wooden made it clear that everyone had a role on the team; individuals had different roles, but there were no subordinates and no labels like "starters" and "subs." Managers were treated as part of the team rather than, as is so common in other teams, as servants to the players. For example, to Wooden, how the team left the dressing room was a matter of pride and of consideration for others. As he proudly notes in his autobiography,

> Many building custodians across the country will tell you that UCLA leaves the shower and dressing room the cleanest of any team. We pick up all the tape, never throw soap on the shower floor for someone to slip on, make sure all showers are turned off, and all towels are accounted for. The towels are always deposited in a receptacle if there is one or stacked neatly near the door.

> It seems to me that this is everyone's responsibility—not just the manager's. Furthermore, I believe it is a form of discipline that should be a way of life, not to please some building custodian, but as an expression of courtesy and politeness that each of us owes to his fellow-man. These little things establish a spirit of togetherness and consideration and help unite the team into a solid unit. (1972, p. 105)

Courtesy, politeness, and consideration developed in players a sense of awareness for the other guy and reinforced the knack for instinctively passing the ball or setting a pick when it was for the good of the team. Sharp commands alone, even from one like Wooden, would not establish such instincts of selflessness and team play. Such instincts had to be nurtured and reinforced with repeated on-court and off-court demonstrations. Players had to be shown convincingly that the end result of consideration and selfless play was the good of the whole team. In turn, the development of

---

*A plaque with these words engraved on it sat on President Reagan's desk throughout his eight years as president.

these instincts redounded to the benefit of the individual players. It made them winners, winners with character, not characters with wins.

Relating to the Players

To successfully achieve sacrifices from gifted grandstanders for the sake of unity, Wooden knew that it was vital to develop a sound relationship both on-court and off-court with his players. When disagreements and questions arose, it was essential that the players not only respected and trusted his judgments, but also knew he was interested in them as individuals.

The bond of trust between athlete and coach is a delicate relationship formed in several ways. Some coaches get deeply involved in the personal lives of their athletes and develop friendships that nurture dedication and trust. Wooden tacked a different course; at the height of Wooden's coaching career, he was too old to effect close friendships with 18- to 20-year-olds. He respected them, but let his players know that they were still immature and had great opportunities ahead to grow and develop. His championship players remember their relationship with him largely as a pupil-teacher experience.

Frankness stands out as one of Wooden's special qualities and styles of relating to his players. Helping them along the road of life was another. As he candidly explained it,

> On the floor, I'm not interested in them as individuals but as a team. Off the floor it's different. Some of them may not realize my interest in them as individuals—at the start—but they later will. (Chapin & Prugh, 1973, p. 302)

> I often tell my players, that next to my own flesh and blood, they are the closest to me. They are my children. I get wrapped up in them, their lives and their problems. (Wooden, 1972, p. 63)

However, showing concern for each individual's welfare, for "their lives and their problems" did not assure or presume early friendship, and Wooden's saintly demeanor could make a sinner uncomfortable (as I can personally attest). The effect of Wooden's nature upon the team was described by Kareem Abdul-Jabbar (Alcindor, 1969) in an article for *Sports Illustrated* written after he'd led the Bruins to three straight national titles. He portrayed Wooden as a decent, superb, honest man—with a blind spot.

> He had this morality thing where you had to be morally right to play. From that attitude came a serious inability on his part to get along with "problem players."

> If they didn't go to Church every Sunday and study for three hours a night and arrive 15 minutes early to practice and nod with every inspiring word the coach said, they were not morally fit to play; they found themselves on the second team. (p. 38)

Many players viewed Wooden as cool and aloof, and all judged him strict. But that in no way impaired his ability to communicate his feelings or convey his personal concern. His special way of assuring his players that he cared about them was demonstrated through advice and wisdom that was solidly based on firmly held principles. In an age when everyone else seemed to question everything, John Wooden remained true to his beliefs. His consistency was a sobering relief to an experimental era and his players knew where he stood on an issue.

His personal example and verbal admonitions were occasionally irritating, however, and Wooden's old-fashioned thinking could fly in the face of a player's own aspirations for personal development and expression. For example, another of Wooden's great stars of the 1970s expressed frustration with him in a *Sports Illustrated* article:

> "Mike Warren, the ex-star black guard of the Bruins, said that Wooden's relationships with blacks 'have no meaning. The coaching staff was seriously interested only in us playing, studying, and keeping out of trouble. Our individual progress in terms of maturing as black men was of no concern. It's all superficial, the same kind of dialogue every day.' " (Chapin & Prugh, 1973, p. 303)

At the time of those remarks, Warren had been dating a white girl, and Wooden had received threatening phone calls about it. He tried to discourage Mike and later said " 'I would discourage anybody from interracial dating, I imagine whites would have trouble dating in an Oriental society too. It's asking for trouble. But I've never told a player who he could or couldn't date' " (Chapin &

Prugh, 1973, p. 303). Warren said that Wooden's advice " 'didn't stop me . . . but how about telling me my life is in danger? How's that for a hint?' " (Chapin & Prugh, 1973, p. 303) His irritation didn't lead to a break in the relationship with his coach, however; Mike Warren knew Wooden's concern was sincere. Mutual appreciation and trust do not require close personal friendship.

Fred Slaughter, the center on UCLA's first championship team who became a member of the UCLA Law School faculty and administration, has provided added perspective on Wooden's race relations. Speaking about his days as a player for Wooden, Slaughter noted that Wooden was " 'really green' " in relating to Black players, but that he did " 'as well as his background let him.' " He further emphasized that Wooden was never openly prejudiced or discriminating; he just didn't understand the Black man in terms of social values, needs, and moods. But Wooden did " 'mature quite a bit in this area' " according to Slaughter, especially after Kareem Abdul-Jabbar and Lucius Allen joined the team. And he adds, " 'I always noticed coach Wooden treating all the players, irregardless of race, as team players, not as White players and Black players' " (Chapin & Prugh, 1973, p. 304).

Black or White, Wooden's interest in his players was first and foremost in their roles as players. This helped him separate himself from his players' personal lives and refrain from making personal judgments about them and their behavior. As Mike Warren noted (Chapin & Prugh, 1973, p. 303), this gave the appearance that he was only interested in his athletes as players and students, and not in their other concerns and desires. This is not to say he did not care about them personally, and in his early career he did get more involved in the lives of his players. But by the late 60s and 70s, he had lessened his involvement. This later strategy—consciously or unconsciously applied—minimized the potential for conflict which was patently immense. When the gifted guard Lucius Allen was arrested for possession of marijuana in the fabled late 60s, Wooden expressed no personal judgement. Allen was young, talented, Black, and angry, and Wooden knew it. When the charges were later dropped, the ordeal didn't affect Wooden's opinion of Lucius as a player.

Bill Walton—White, idealistic, and politically active—came to UCLA as the second Abdul-Jabbar. He, too, except for basketball, had little in common with Wooden. In May 1972, Walton sat down in the middle of Wilshire Boulevard in rush hour traffic to protest the Vietnam War. Wooden handled the arrest philosophically. As he'd said before, "Stand up for what you believe but be willing to accept the consequences." Later, Walton asked for Wooden's permission to smoke marijuana, saying he'd heard it might relieve the pain in his knees. Wooden responded negatively, " 'I'm no doctor, but I know it's against the law' " (Wolff, 1989).

However, restraining himself strictly to the coach-player relationship did not insure Wooden against conflict. His players often challenged him, testing his resolve. As Alexander Wolff (1989) reported,

> Former UCLA center Steve Patterson remembers the day, in the fall of 1970, that he and forward Sidney Wicks asked to be excused from practice to show solidarity with a nationwide rally protesting the Vietnam War. "He asked us if this reflected our convictions, and we told him it did," says Patterson. "He told us he had his convictions, too, and if we missed practice it would be the end of our careers at UCLA.

> We blinked. I don't think he was necessarily unsympathetic to the statement we wanted to make. He may even have agreed with us. But I see the connection. I didn't at the time, but I do now. He continually challenged you about your attitude toward the team as a whole. He set the standards. He didn't let us set the standards, even though we wanted to." (p. 96)

Although Wooden's rules for his players remained basically unchanged, his interpretation of them became more flexible with time. Some examples of Wooden's flexibility involved drinking and smoking. There was a time in his coaching career when smoking or drinking during the season would have been cause for automatic dismissal. But by the late 1960s, he didn't tell his players that, rather he admonished them to recognize their stature and the impact of their example on others. "I tell them that because they are in the public eye and are seen wherever they go and whatever they do they should feel obligated to set a good example for admiring youngsters" (Wooden, 1972, p. 71).

But Wooden didn't bend on profanity. He wouldn't tolerate it—a slip, okay, but not repeated swearing. He viewed it as insubordination as well as disrespectful bad behavior. First offenses would lead to dismissal from the day's practice—repeated offenses from the team, although reinstatement was likely with an appropriate apology. He was equally strict regarding rules on appropriate appearance. Dress was allowed to become more casual, hair longer, and rules on curfew and discipline more lax, but Wooden maintained certain limits, despite mind-boggling risks.

> Under the rules, organized practice cannot be held until October 15, but press and picture day may be scheduled one day earlier. One year, and I won't say what year, one of our stars came with extra long sideburns, one with a goatee, and another with mutton chops to draw their game equipment. Always on hand for this, I just stopped them, looked at my watch, and said: "You have twenty minutes to decide whether you're going to play basketball at UCLA this year or not. There are clippers and razors in the training room."
>
> "You'll be crucified," one of them said.
>
> "That may well be, but you won't be around to see it."
>
> They decided in a hurry. Well within the allotted time they were back and passed inspection. Later they kidded me about it occasionally, and all of them at one time or another tried to find out what they'd been afraid to test me on earlier. "You really wouldn't have stuck to it, would you, coach?"
>
> "You'll never really know, will you?" My reply still didn't commit me. "I'm the only one who really knows that."
>
> Once during the summer when his hair was quite long, another very prominent player asked me, "What would you do if I refused to have my hair cut?"
>
> "I won't do anything."
>
> "I thought you wouldn't let us wear our hair real long."
>
> "I won't. It's quite all right; you can wear your hair any way you want. I can't determine how long you wear your hair. All I can determine is whether or not you play."
>
> "I thought there was a catch," he said, as my words sank in.
>
> "That's right." (Wooden, 1972, pp. 164-165)

In short, Wooden did bend with the times, but only a modest amount. Yet he held and commanded his players' trust by conveying sincere concern. He could be cool and aloof, but never superficial. Wooden harbored no pretense of controlling his players' lives—he knew the futility of that. He merely set the rules. The players themselves decided whether or not to abide by them, and, consequently, whether or not to play at UCLA.

Wooden's Wisdom

It was these and other lessons on life that made Wooden's players listen to him and learn to play for the good of the team. Indeed, it was precisely because he could draw parallels between basketball and life that he had such an advantage over his players whenever disagreement on lineups or style of play occurred. Bart Starr (1972), Lombardi's famous Green Bay Packer quarterback, compared Wooden's influence to that of his own beloved coach:

> What he's [Wooden's] done year in and year out over the past decade is fabulous. He continues to win because he has something going for those young men that will help sustain them for the rest of their lives. His philosophy is very much the same as Coach Vince Lombardi's was. Coach Wooden equates basketball to the game of life. He says you have to be unselfish, that you have to play for the good of the team, that you have to be disciplined and do what he wants you to do as a team, that he will tolerate no individuality within that team. He wants you to play as a unit. This is really what you end up doing in life because sooner or later you end up on a team. (p. 93)

A typical example of the Wooden wisdom that heightened the players' respect for him was his advice on how to deal with all the winning. Whereas Wooden, basketball, and winning are nearly synonymous to us, it is a oddity, but true, that "winning" was a word Wooden himself seldom used. Wooden's teams didn't *beat* opponents, they *outscored* them. His de-emphasis of winning has been commented on many times by his players. Here are three examples (all are cited in Wooden, 1984).

> • Before a game, the thing that always impressed me, that could take a lot of pressure off me as a player, was that he never challenged us to win the game. He always challenged us to do the best we could do. To walk into the locker room when the game was over, look in the mirror, and say to myself,

Walt Hazzard, I did the best that I could do tonight.—*Walt Hazzard*

- He didn't talk about winning. We all want to win, but he talked about as long as you can do the best that you can with what you got, I'm gonna be happy about it. And you should be happy about it.—*Eddie Sheldrake*

- I played on teams under him that won 73 games in a row and never once did he say "Let's go out and win this one." He never made a big deal about it, he always said before the game "All I ask is that after the game you leave the floor with your heads up." When I look back on some of the things that happened under him, it is just simply awesome.—*Jamaal Wilkes*

How did Wooden and his players not get spoiled or sidetracked once the wins began pouring in? Wooden (1972) had recognized the problem explicitly.

It is difficult sometimes to reach a team that is so weighted with experience. Most of them had been on two national championship teams and had already been labeled by sportswriters and sportscasters for a third. These were big, strong, experienced players who knew they were big, strong, and experienced players. It was difficult to keep them from becoming complacent. My hardest job all year was to fight the "I-can-get-the-job-done-when-I-turn-it-on" attitude and to keep them striving to improve. (p. 172)

Besides goading his players to strive for improvement Wooden challenged his players to view the positive positively. In the early 1970s, Wooden reported

"One of the things I said in my annual letter to this year's team is that it was going to be more difficult for them because they would be expected to win. Some might consider it an unenviable position but I told them I consider it an enviable position . . . a mark of respect they had earned. I also told them that the past is history and that nothing that happened in the past can change or affect what they were going to do in the future. What you did yesterday, that's gone by. You can do something about today, so you must think in those terms.

"I don't believe the sign on [UCLA Athletic Director] J.D. Morgan's desk—WINNING SOLVES ALL PROBLEMS. I'm

John Wooden and his 1969 NCAA Champions. Many of the players are multiple time champs, as indicated by the number of fingers raised.

more inclined toward what Charlie Brown says in the comics: Winning ain't everything but losing is nothing.

"I've pretty well been able to adopt the philosophy I've had—to embrace the Pyramid of success pretty well. I believe that we have 'won'—that is, accomplished all we're capable of accomplishing—when we've *lost* games.

"No I don't think we've created a monster by winning so much. Rather than calling what we've achieved a dynasty, I prefer to think of it as a cycle. And I believe all cycles come to an end." (Chapin & Prugh, 1973, p. 308)

Like Father, Like Son

Wooden was an excellent teacher to be sure, but he would credit his teaching skills to his philosophy; and his coaching was as rigorous, optimistic, and strict as his philosophy. He credited much of his devotion to profound issues to his father, whom he profoundly loved and admired. Indeed, Wooden (1967) attributed to his father much of his own personal creed.

Inside my wallet is a piece of paper which I have handled so many times it is worn and ragged. It was given me by my father when I graduated from the eighth grade of an old country school in Centerton, Indiana.

My father in his simple way was a most remarkable man. Although we had few material possessions on our farm, Dad was a man who believed that one needed a philosophy of life if he were to amount to anything. On the paper he gave me for graduation, Dad had listed the following creed, which he had entitled "Seven Things To Do":

1. To thine own self be true, and it must follow, as the night the day, thou canst not then be false to any man.
2. Make each day your masterpiece.
3. Live each day as it should be lived. Never leave until tomorrow what can be done today.
4. Help others. A perfect life can be lived in helping others.
5. Drink deeply from good books. One book alone would suffice—the Bible.
6. Don't take friendship for granted. Study friendship and make it a fine art.
7. Most important of all, pray for guidance each day and Divine guidance will come in some way.

I've found these guides to be meaningful in every phase of my life. During the 18 years I have coached basketball at UCLA, they have helped me develop a balanced attitude toward victory and defeat. We play to win, of course, but more important to me is what the boys learn about life. That is why I stress the same principles Dad did. (p. 29)

To conclude, Wooden's remarkable success stemmed primarily from his values and his consistency in living by those values. He abided by his pyramid. He was not sidetracked by the passing glories of triumphs, many as there were. He was selfless in example and in demeanor. He enjoyed the simple daily routine of hard purposeful work. And he took pride in it. Money was incidental— his highest annual salary was $32,500 in 1975. Lavish offers did not detour him. As he noted, the greatest gains from his work are expressed in one of his favorite poems:

THEY ASK ME WHY I TEACH
by Glennice L. Harmon

They ask me why I teach,
And I reply,
Where could I find more splendid company?
There sits a statesman,
Strong, unbiased, wise,
Another later Webster,
Silver-tongued.
And there a doctor
Whose quick, steady hand
Can mend a bone,
Or stem the lifeblood's flow.
A builder sits beside him—
Upward rise
The arches of a church he builds, wherein
That minister will speak the word of God,
And lead a stumbling soul to touch the Christ.
And all about
A lesser gathering
Of farmers, merchants, teachers,
Laborers, men
Who work and vote and build
And plan and pray
Into a great tomorrow.
And I say,
"I may not see the church,
Or hear the word,
Or eat the food their hands will grow."
And yet—I may.
And later I may say,
"I knew the lad,
And he was strong,
Or weak, or kind, or proud.
Or bold, or gay.
I knew him once,
But then he was a boy."
They ask me why I teach, and I reply,
"Where could I find more splendid company?"

Rather than his winning record, Wooden's greatest achievement was his gift to others, his teachings on how to find the best in oneself and how to find peace of mind. UCLA won championship after championship because of ideas. Most of his players (and others) came to realize this eventually. As Wooden (1984) said,

> I would talk to them about the Pyramid once a year and invite them to come in and talk to me about any aspect of it that they so desired. And very few would come in.

> But very few have failed to come in and talk to me about it some years after they graduated. And that . . . that always pleased me.

Wooden guided the youth and in return was rewarded with pleasing, splendid company and peace of mind.

John Wooden's Honors

Here is a list of some of the honors Wooden received personally during his illustrious career as player and coach.

1930-32—All-America basketball player at Purdue

1932—College Basketball "Player of the Year"
—Big Ten Medal for Proficiency in Scholarship and Athletics (Awarded to graduating athlete with outstanding grades)

1943—All-Time All-American Basketball Team, Helms Athletic Foundation

1960—National Basketball Hall of Fame (as a player)

1964—Indiana Basketball Hall of Fame (in first group)
—California "Father of the Year"

1964-67-69-70-72-73—College "Coach of the Year"

1970—*Sporting News* "Sports' Man of the Year"

1971—Friars Club "Coach of the Century"

1972—National Basketball Hall of Fame (as a coach—only person inducted in more than one category)

1973—*Sports Illustrated* "Sportsman of the Year"
—Whitney M. Young, Jr., National Urban League Memorial Award for Humanitarism

—UCLA Honorary "Alumnus of the Year"

—Campbell College "Honorary Doctor of Humanities"

1974—First Annual Dr. James Naismith Peach Basket Award (for outstanding contributions to basketball)

—First Annual National Layman's Leadership Institute Velvet Covered Brick Award for Christian Leadership

As is plainly evidenced above, Coach Wooden has been honored for many things besides his ability as one of basketball's all-time greatest coaches.

John Wooden's Head Coaching Record

11-Season High School Coaching Record (Two seasons at Dayton, KY, High School and nine seasons at South Bend, IN, Central High School).

	Won	Lost	Percent
11-season totals	218	42	.838

2-Season Coaching Record at Indiana State University in Terre Haute, IN

	Won	Lost	Percent
1946-47	18	7	.720
1947-48	29	7	.806
Totals	47	14	.778

27-Season Coaching Record at UCLA

Conference				Full season			
Year	Won	Lost	Percent	Year	Won	Lost	Percent
1949*	10	2	.714	1948-49	22	7	.759
1950**	10	2	.714	1949-50	24	7	.774
1951*	9	4	.692	1950-51	19	10	.655
1952**	8	4	.667	1951-52	19	12	.613
1953	6	6	.500	1952-53	16	8	.667
1954	7	5	.583	1953-54	18	7	.720
1955*	11	1	.917	1954-55	21	5	.808
1956**	16	0	1.000	1955-56	22	6	.785
1957	13	3	.819	1956-57	22	4	.846
1958	10	6	.625	1957-58	16	10	.615
1959	10	6	.625	1958-59	16	9	.640
1960	7	5	.583	1959-60	14	12	.538
1961	7	5	.583	1960-61	18	8	.692
1962***	10	2	.833	1961-62	18	11	.621
1963****	8	5	.615	1962-63	20	9	.690
1964*****	15	0	1.000	1963-64	30	0	1.000
1965*****	14	0	1.000	1964-65	28	2	.933
1966	10	4	.714	1965-66	18	8	.692
1967*****	14	0	1.000	1966-67	30	0	1.000
1968*****	14	0	1.000	1967-68	29	1	.967
1969*****	13	1	.928	1968-69	29	1	.967
1970*****	12	2	.857	1969-70	28	2	.933

(Cont.)

John Wooden's Head Coaching Record (Continued)

27-Season Coaching Record at UCLA

Conference				Full season			
Year	Won	Lost	Percent	Year	Won	Lost	Percent
1971*****	14	0	1.000	1970-71	29	1	.967
1972*****	14	0	1.000	1971-72	30	0	1.000
1973*****	14	0	1.000	1972-73	30	0	1.000
1974***	12	2	.857	1973-74	26	4	.867
1975*****	12	2	.857	1974-75	28	3	.903
Totals	316	68	.823	Totals	620	147	.808

40-Season All-Time Coaching Record

	Won	Lost	Percent
40-season totals	885	203	.813

*Pacific Coast Conference, Southern Division, Champions
**PCC Champions
***Pacific-8 Champions; NCAA Far West Regional Champions
****Pacific-8 Champions, defeated Stanford in playoff game for berth in NCAA
  Far West Regional Playoffs
*****Pacific-8 Champions; NCAA Champions

Chapter 4

James "Doc" Counsilman: From Human Needs to World Records

The Spitz Factor

At one time or another, most parents dream of the kind of life Adele and Arnold Spitz actually lived as parents. Their handsome, athletically gifted son, Mark, took to the water as if born aquatic. From the age of seven, when Mark first entered a YMCA swimming program near his home in Sacramento, his destiny as a world champion was predicted. The next year Mark's parents took him to Coach Sherm Chavoor at the famed Arden Hills Swim Club.

"Doc" recording times of his swimmers.

Visiting the pool, his dad asked Mark, "How many lanes in the pool?" "Six," his son replied. "How many lanes win, Mark?" he asked. "One," Mark answered. It was a father and son routine they repeated many times.

By the age of 10, Mark held 17 national age-group swimming records. Seemingly never satisfied, the Spitz family moved three times in twice as many years, usually to find a better coach. When Mark was 14, they moved to the South Bay so Mark could swim under George Haines at the Santa Clara Swim Club. The payoff was several world records set by Mark at the age of 17. Then came the 1968 Olympic Games in Mexico City. There he won four medals: two gold, one silver, and a bronze. But he disappointed an insatiable public and an unsympathetic press who had touted him for more. As the press scoffed, the Spitz family pondered, then pressed forward. Their game plan, true to form, was get the best coach in the country.

Though Mark was the hottest prospect in college swimming in 1968, every coach considered him the personal property of Coach Don Gambril of Long Beach State. Young Spitz, however, was wavering. He had personally witnessed the power of Indiana University's legendary Coach James "Doc" Counsilman. The U.S. 1968 Olympic Swimming Team included eight IU swimmers. Based on comparative times, if Counsilman's IU team had competed as a nation in 1968, it would have beaten the world. When "Doc" took his team to Fort Lauderdale over Christmas vacation that year, they found Mark wandering around the pool. His presence was no coincidence. He had purposely arranged the surprise rendezvous.

California kids aren't easily convinced to migrate to the Midwest. Suntans fade there. The winters are too long and cold, the summers too drab and humid, and the brief springs are barely detectable in between. But there was no doubt in Doc's mind that Indiana University was the right place for Mark, tan and all. For Doc knew exactly what to do to help Mark rebound from his demoralized state and refocus his energies. He also knew to be prudently cautious. On seeing Mark, he said "Hey Mark, when do you start school in Long Beach?" Mark replied, "Well, I haven't made up my mind." Still Doc held back, until Mark said "I'd be interested in coming to Indiana." Then Doc asked Mark to visit Bloomington. He accepted; but shortly before returning to California, Mark slipped on some ice. According to Counsilman, he "fell on his butt.

I thought we had lost him right there." But Mark had a bigger fall to make up for, and he chose IU (Sutton, 1990, p. C-12).

Under Doc's canny tutelage, Mark realized Olympic heights unmatched by any human. At the Munich Games in the summer of 1972, Mark capped his senior year at IU by winning seven Olympic gold medals while simultaneously setting seven world records. Under Counsilman, Mark Spitz became the greatest swimmer in the history of the sport. Counsilman's praise of Spitz's talent was double-barrelled. He called him, "the most talented swimmer in the world ever" (Sutton, 1990, p. C-12), and "the most talented swimmer we (IU) ever had" (Novak, 1990, p. 7).

Counsilman has gratefully acknowledged his good fortune in attracting Spitz to IU many times, for as he has often said, "The main thing that makes a good coach is good athletes" (Novak, 1990, p. 7). Nevertheless, it is also evident that Doc's legendary coaching record did not depend on Spitz alone. He also coached such world record greats as Gary Hall (twice World Swimmer of the year), Chet Jastremski, Charlie Hickox (Associated Press selection for most outstanding athlete of the 1968 Olympics), John Kinsella (Sullivan Award winner), Mike Stamm, Don McKinzie, Jim Montgomery, Frank McKinny, Jr., and hundreds of other world class swimmers.

"Doc" with Don McKenzie (left), Mark Spitz (center), and Charlie Hickox (right) at Royer Pool.

When I moved to Bloomington and joined the economics faculty at Indiana University in 1971, basketball coach Bobby Knight was on the rise, but it was Counsilman who was king of IU's athletic world as well as the world of swimming. As Knight said upon Counsilman's retirement: " 'I don't think there has ever been a coach in any American collegiate sport that has done more for his sport or more thoroughly dominated his sport than Doc Counsilman' " (cited in Isaacson, 1990, pp. 3-10). Although Counsilman insists that he won with world class swimmers, Knight and others know that he alone attracted them; he alone trained them. Overall, he coached 58 Olympians at IU, and won 287 meets in 33 years against only 37 losses. Beginning in 1968, the year before Spitz joined his team, Counsilman ran off a string of six straight NCAA Championships.* In his career at IU, Doc Counsilman claimed 23 Big Ten titles, 20 of them consecutively from 1961 to 1980; he had 18 undefeated seasons, 12 in a row from 1967 to 1978.

Commitment to Continued Learning

Indisputably, the key to Counsilman's program and his coaching success was his commitment to continued learning. He was committed not only to the pursuit of knowledge, but to its advancement. He helped build a pathway of progress that his athletes could follow.

His natural curiosity was a main building block, and as Counsilman (1968) said

The human pursuit of knowledge seems to follow a three-phase pattern: The first phase is curiosity which comes when the person's interest is aroused and he begins to look at things, it is to be hoped, with some degree of objectivity; the second phase is that of confusion which comes about when the person

---

*It merits emphasis that the number should be much higher; perhaps as high as ten. By most swimming authorities' accounts Indiana had the best teams in the county in 1961, 62, and 63, but IU swimmers were not permitted to compete in the NCAA championships: the NCAA had imposed a blanket probation on IU because of the football team's recruiting transgressions. In 1961 Michigan won the NCAA title in swimming but had been previously beaten by Indiana. In 1962 IU won the Big Ten by a mile—and Ohio State won the NCAA. On their return to the NCAA Championships in 1964, the IU team was touted to win but lost to USC by four points (91-95).

is unable to analyze the situation immediately and sees no possible answer to the question or sees the possibility of several answers; the third phase is that of the search for the answer or the quest for knowledge. This is the never-ending phase, the one that will always keep man busy.

The true scientist is curious. He is able to recognize the problem he is confused about, and often his confusion is what keeps him in search of the truth. In athletics, the intelligent coach and athlete are constantly searching for new approaches and improved methods. These are the people who advance our sport. Other people, less inspired and creative, adopt their techniques. (p. viii)

Doc viewed himself a scientist, not the test tube stereotype but one similarly committed to the scientific approach. He was strongly impressed by the inscription in the foyer of the Science Building of the Seattle World's Fair of 1962.

To learn about the world around him, a scientist must ask, observe, suppose, experiment, and analyze:

In asking—the right question must be posed.

In observing—the significant must be distinguished from the unimportant.

In supposing—a workable answer (or hypothesis) may be predicted, but a scientist must be ready to abandon it.

In experimenting—the right instrument must be chosen or borrowed from the tool kit of some other branch of science.

In analyzing—the scientist must, with his mind and his imagination, draw conclusions from the data his research has revealed.

To sustain his progress as a scientist coach Doc persistently asked himself motivating questions:

Am I constantly observing objectively, evaluating, and reevaluating, or have I reached the point where I look, but am not aware of what I see?

Am I supposing or trying to find a workable answer for the problems which confront me. Once I arrive at a conclusion, am I then inflexible or do I always keep an open mind?

Am I experimenting? If possible, do I use tools from other areas of science such as motion pictures, physiological tests, and psychological tests. Do I also use tests within my area; tests of strength, flexibility, agility? In experimenting, do I, within reasonable limits, try new ideas, that is, isometric contractions, and so on?

In analyzing, am I arriving at logical conclusions or are my conclusions colored by prejudice, inadequate thinking, poor background, and lack of imagination? (1968, p. viii)

Doc's athletes knew that he was not only on top of the most advanced techniques of the sport, but that he was also a prime mover in advancing the sport; they were his guinea pigs. His widely used books on swimming, his most important one translated into 20 languages, unselfishly spelled out for others the training advances he had discovered. Never once did he attempt to hoard an advance for his own team's special advantage. As several of his swimmers proudly told me, he gave his specialized knowledge away every time.

Doc was driven with curiosity and emphatically said "The minute your curiosity dies, you're finished as far as any creative effort is concerned" (Cecil, 1978). Taking as his example the training of runners in the 1950s, he introduced swimming to interval training—workouts of specified distances with brief measured rests between the paced distances. Before Counsilman pioneered interval training in swimming, the athletes all did overdistance, hours of it, over and over daily. The monotony was deadening. Interval training adds variety, and enables swimmers to set certain goals such as times per lap on repeated intervals, and to watch the clock to check on themselves. Interval training permitted Doc to develop practice sessions where he urged his swimmers past the extremes of stress for brief periods. His system became known as the "hurt, pain, agony" concept.

At about the same time that Doc introduced interval training to swimming, he invented a huge poolside pace clock in his cellar. The first one was for his swimmers. Then he made others and sold them to schools like Army, Navy, and Princeton. He even invented the pool bottom lane markers now used in pools worldwide.

Counsilman's earliest research on swimming strokes focused largely on the Bernouillis principle, and he discovered that swimmers do not propel themselves forward simply by pushing water back. In consequence, one technique he introduced was a method of snapping the hands and using an uneven stroke, rather than an even, steady, smooth stroke. He employed endless film footage—shooting his own athletes, often underwater—to display and explain the gains from adopting such new methods.

The showcase of athlete science at Royer Pool was the weight room, where Doc personally designed each piece of equipment. His weights were not barbells, but rather specially designed weights to accommodate forces like inertia. His designs eliminated those inertia forces that interfere with the effectiveness of weight-lifting exercises to strengthen muscles. His applications, the first of their kind to training machines, were based on isokinetic theory.

A short exemplary story of legendary proportions stems from the early 70s when Bobby Knight told Doc about his talented center Kent Benson who then had a low vertical jump. Doc suggested designing an isokinetic machine into what he called the "Leaper." Kent worked all summer on the machine and raised his vertical jump from 22 to 27 inches. Knight's team, with Benson at the pivot, later won the NCAA championship.

In the late 70s, Doc invented the biokinetic bench, used around the world today to imitate stroke mechanics, and many other

"Doc" demonstrating the stroke mechanics of the breaststroke.

Counsilman inventions and contributions could be listed. But these products of his insatiably curious mind matter less than his attitude about learning. According to his colleague, the IU diving coach Hobie Billingsley, Doc's mind was infectious: " 'He's such an interesting guy. He can talk to you about a light bulb and make it interesting. He's so well read and he's intelligent as hell. I never sit down with him that I don't get excited about what he's talking about' " (Sutton, 1990, p. C-12).

No Sure Bet

Where Doc found the curiosity and motivation to adopt the scientist-scholar approach to athletics is a curiosity itself. Born in 1920, Counsilman lived through the Great Depression destitute. He was fatherless from the age of two, and, although his mother wanted him to be a doctor, he didn't achieve much in his early schooling. He didn't think he was smart enough, and his ragged clothes portrayed a dead-end kid, the kind you didn't bother with.

Looking back, Doc recalls: " 'I hated school. I graduated at the bottom one percent of my class. . . . But swimming was something I could excel at. I always loved the pool, and my (YMCA) coach was a true role model for me—a real father figure' " (Novak, 1990, p. 7). The coach who helped young Counsilman was Ernst Vornbrock of the St. Louis Downtown YMCA Swimming Team. As Doc tells it, " 'I met (Vornbrock) my senior year in high school. Then I went to college when I was 21, and I graduated in the top one percent . . . he changed my attitude toward my self esteem, and my self image was improved. It was more than just coaching swimming' " (Silverstein, 1989, p. 20).

Once Counsilman found self-esteem and got his break, he never let go of the advantage. That break came in 1941 when he entered Ohio State at age 21. In those days there were no scholarships, but OSU helped land him a job earning 40¢ an hour as an elevator operator in the state office building. It was enough to live on, and that year he won the national championship in the butterfly-breast stroke. Two years later, in 1943, he set the world record in that event, but had his college life at OSU interrupted when he was drafted into the Army Air Corps. After earning a distinguished combat record as a B-24 bomber pilot in Europe, he returned to Ohio State, at age 25, to captain the swimming team. Because of his age, maturity, experience, and skill, the other swimmers often sought his advice. He evolved into a mentor and this experience along with that gained from his old coach from St. Louis fostered his interest in coaching and in building his own philosophy of coaching.

His desire for more formal education, however, propelled him onward to graduate school, first to the University of Illinois to study physiology, then to the University of Iowa in 1948 to continue his studies and to work as an assistant swimming coach. James Counsilman gained his nickname "Doc" in 1951 upon receiving his doctorate in physiology. But in reality, his added name was earned in life. His learning and teachings progressed over the years while he coached at Indiana University from 1957 to 1990, and the name "Doc" stuck because of his commitment to continued learning.

Doc's Philosophy of Coaching

Doc's mentor, Ernie Vornbrock, had conducted his swimming program in St. Louis in ways Doc viewed as very special. As Doc said, "It was more than swimming." Vornbrock took 17-year-old

"Doc" giving a lecture to his swimmers.

Counsilman under his wing and literally turned his life around. Vornbrock's aim was to help all his swimmers gain personal and social fulfillment. He made it clear to them that his primary obligation to them was in the larger sense—to assist them to achieve their potential academically and socially as well as athletically.

Although Doc knew the futility of personality imitation, he valued his coach's example and wanted to be appreciated by his own athletes the way he had appreciated Vornbrock. This motivated him to build his own philosophy of coaching around needs that are basic to all humans. He borrowed his philosophy from Maslow's hierarchy of human needs and adapted it to the context of a coach and athlete competitive team situation. He constantly reminded himself what it was that his swimmers needed from him and his program. And the following were the eight basic elements of Doc's personal philosophy of helping his swimmers on a day to day basis.

1. Love and Affection

Doc recognized the importance of being liked and wanted his swimmers to know that he had a genuine affection for them. He took a deep personal interest in them. He knew their studies and pinned to memory their grade point averages, best swimming times, and best workouts; he knew their goals and aspirations, their girlfriends, and their problems. Here's a typical example of how Doc showed he really cared, as reported by Dick Denny (1968):

> Counsilman is never too busy for his swimmers, star or supporting member. He has the amazing faculty of being able to converse with an interviewer intently and at the same time watch the huge clock on the opposite side of the pool by which the swimmers time themselves.
>
> When the interviewer is least expecting it, Counsilman might break in and yell, "That's good, Bob, very good. That's your best of the year."
>
> Re-engaging the interviewer, Counsilman says, "You have to watch the times and know their best ones. A fellow may have a very good workout and if you miss it, he's really down. You can't let that happen."

Doc also hungered for affection in return; he cherished strong ties to former athletes and was pleased to learn when lifelong friendships were sustained among teammates. He viewed such lifelong friendships as one of the greatest benefits of competitive team sports.

He believed it was best that athletes like their coach, and if not, at least respect him. After winning another NCAA championship in the mid-1970s he said, "If your athletes don't like you, you should take time off to find out why" (Denny, 1968).

Finally, as Doc wisely understood, displays of affection should never be counterfeit or feigned; flattery will be detected and could be ruinous.

Doc's caring for his swimmers was genuine. Pete Andersen, an unknown freshman walk-on at IU, became the year's third-best American in the breaststroke in 1962 because of Doc. Pete tells how Doc never set himself apart:

> He was always with you, like the time at Yale at the 1964 NCAA's when we lost to USC 91-95. We had no money and Doc and Hobie and all of us slept on couches and cots in makeshift dormitories. Then came the disappointing loss at ten o'clock Saturday night. We left immediately in a pounding rain, and Doc did most of the driving on our twelve-hour return. He sacrificed with us every inch of the way and that was typical of Doc. We worked hard, but he was with us working just as hard or, by example, even harder. (personal communication, September 30, 1990)

2. Security

As a youngster, Counsilman got his disproportionate share of insecurity. The Great Depression impressed on him and his whole generation the importance of security, food, a job, a place to sleep, and so on. Doc tells of an experience in 1938 in St. Louis where, before going to swimming practice each day at the YMCA, he would spend several futile hours in the employment lines trying to land a job. More often than not he'd arrive at the pool bitter and depressed. Vornbrock, his coach, would always give him a friendly greeting; "Hiya Jim, how are things going today?"—his big smile beaming. Young Counsilman was skeptical at first, even cynical, saying to himself, "What's he so happy about? I wish he wouldn't give me that phony smile." As he tells it,

One day I came in as usual and Ernie didn't notice me for a while, and when he did, he only greeted me in an off-hand way. I said to myself, "What in the hell is wrong with him? He sure got up on the wrong side of the bed." A couple of days later I walked into the pool and got the old enthusiastic "Hiya, Jim" and the smile I had thought was so phony. This time I said to myself, "Thank God he's got himself straightened out." (1977, p. 258)

Doc learned two lessons from this experience that would help him in the future. First, Vornbrock taught him the importance of a positive attitude, either purposely or unintentionally, Doc was never sure. Second, those earlier days helped Counsilman to understand the pain of insecurity in college life and how to help overcome it.

Consider the average freshman student in a large school of several thousand students. He goes from class to class, seeing very few people he knows. He deals with many people whom he knows only casually. He finds himself in a new and strange environment where the leader of the group is someone he has never met. The students in his class are competing with him for grades. He may lack status in the group, he feels insecure. He goes to the pool for a workout. He walks in the door and the coach greets him with a "Hiya, Jim, how are things going?" and gives him a smile. He is in a familiar environment where he knows what to expect. He belongs to the group and is accepted by the team members. He can predict that the coach will be enthusiastic and have a positive attitude. He also knows that the coach is an emotionally stable, mature individual. What a feeling of security these factors generate! (1977, p. 254)

As Doc saw it, a moody coach with emotional highs and lows is bewildering to young athletes. Such a person creates an atmosphere of worry, fear, anxiety, and resentment and shouldn't be in coaching. Indeed, these personalities are hard to deal with in any profession, but when teammanship is important such personal characteristics are disastrous.

3. Status

Each of us participates in groups throughout life: in families, clubs, teams, religious groups, social groups, student bodies, communities, professions, nations, and the world. We are all conscious of our standings in these groups, and, taken together, these rankings determine our overall personal status. Our struggle for status and to elevate our self-image is part of our competitive world. As Doc saw it:

The Swimmer is a member of his team, he is also a member of the student body and probably of many other groups. He may have the lowest rank order on your team, but his membership on the team may raise his status in the student body. Thus he has raised his status in one group merely by being a member of another. This is especially true if the team is successful and has high prestige. If you want to help your swimmers achieve high status, give them a good program in order that they may be successful. Then make sure they receive recognition of their success in the form of publicity, awards, trips, and anything else you can think of. (1977, pp. 254-255)

Doc labored hard to make everyone on the team feel a part of Indiana's great swimming program. He regularly held group dinners for all team members, serving his wife's famed lasagna. Nightly he had individual athletes to his home for dinner, as part of the family. In workouts and performances he watched everyone with equal intensity. Everyone on the team gained status by being important to him and to the program. As his swimmers repeatedly emphasized, Doc had the great ability to make them feel like the most important people in the pool. Everyone came away with that feeling, whether he was a star or a walk-on.

4. Achievement

Within each human resides the desire to achieve whatever he undertakes. It is the coach's responsibility to see that his program provides the swimmers with a feeling of accomplishment, even of creativity. After a practice session in the pool, a workout in the exercise room, or a stroke lecture in the classroom, the swimmer should feel he has made progress towards a goal. In this feeling of accomplishment, the coach must educate him concerning the theories of training. This information about the physiology of training will stimulate him to work more conscientiously than if he is merely following orders. (Counsilman, 1977, p. 255)

Counsilman discovered that the athletes' sense of achievement is heightened and made more clear when they can evaluate for themselves what has been achieved. Coaches should emphasize not just faster times, but an understanding of what has caused improvement, both the *why* and the *how* of practice sessions and techniques. When athletes understand why they are progressing, and not just how to follow a workout schedule, their understanding makes them more cooperative and motivated in workouts.

Another important step in building a sense of achievement is the setting of goals that are compatible with the athletes' own abilities. A coach or a leader who sets unrealistically high goals or performance standards too easily achieved will lose the athletes' confidence. Clearly the need for achievement will be fulfilled only if there is ample one-on-one communication between coach and athlete. That personal communication must be sustained and goals altered as the athlete matures and abilities change.

5. The Group Instinct

Doc strongly believes that almost all individuals, if properly handled, are team oriented. Most of us possess what psychologists refer to as the group instinct. To address this need the coach must foster team spirit and forge strong ties both among the athletes and between each athlete and the coach. This is accomplished by setting goals for all the team members to achieve together, such as winning a certain meet.

The dual human motives of self-interest and group instinct sometimes conflict, and their management requires insight and tact from the coach. Doc tells an interesting story of one of his young stars who was too immature to maintain a proper perspective on the importance of group orientation, although he needed it badly.

He wanted all the headlines, all the world records, to win all the races and get all the glory. He swam poorly on relays in order to save himself for his individual events. He talked only of himself and took no interest in the older swimmers on the team. He was so concerned with fulfilling his needs that he failed to an unnatural degree to consider the needs of anyone else. Yet, in common with us all, he shared the need to be part of a group—which in this case was the team—to be liked and respected. His immaturity lay in the fact that he failed to recognize that he had to help others satisfy their needs to best satisfy his own. Owning all the world records would fail to make a person happy if he knew no one cared for him. Our team member was unhappy, but he had no inkling of the reason why. . . . I told him that he had to take an interest in other people, had to consider their feelings, had to talk about them. Specifically, we decided that he could begin by being interested in the swimming times of his teammates. He could put out on relays and not just be concerned with how he swam in the individual events, in practice, and in meets. He could try congratulating the swimmers when they did well. I told him to remember the word "TATNAM"—"Talk about them, not about me." I gave him a dollar-fifty paperback copy of Dale Carnegie's *How to Win Friends and Influence People*. . . . designed to teach people how to fulfill the needs of others while satisfying their own.

After reading this book, the swimmer made no overnight transition, and often he found it hard to adopt the proper mechanics of behavior. Eventually, he developed a more mature attitude and was accepted by the team. He became happier and better adjusted in all aspects of his life and was able to break the cycle of behavior that had plagued him for so long. He became part of the group, his self-esteem increased and gradually affected all his relationships beneficially. (1977, p. 252)*

The strengthening of team spirit, according to Doc, should always be achieved by positive means. Negative approaches, such as the use of hate psychology focused on another team or other athletes, were taboo with Doc. He felt that hatred was the worst form of motivation, lacked a moral basis, and belonged in no one's sports philosophy.

Doc always made it clear to his athletes that the team was their team, not the coach's team; it belonged to all, the swimmers, the managers, the assistants, as well as the coach. To heighten team spirit, he allowed a fair amount of decision making by the athletes. Many key decisions were made by elected team captains and

---

*Counsilman thoughtfully did not specify the individual's name, but those close to IU swimming in the years of Counsilman's greatest dominance knew unequivocally who he was talking about. The young athlete went on to enjoy a successful, enviable life.

leaders and some by the team as a whole. But Doc recognized that a coach must be careful not to become too permissive, or risk losing authority. "An authoritarian coach who permits the athletes no voice in decision-making is as bad as the overly permissive coach who never disciplines and sometimes doesn't seem to care enough to rebuke bad behavior" (1977, p. 256).

6. Recognition

It's probably fair to say that most of Doc's athletes were blessed with above average ability and had egos to match. Essential to any hard-working athlete is recognition, and a prudent coach will strive to assure that progress and performances are properly recognized. Doc labored to help obtain recognition for his athletes through the sports pages, radio, and television, and he made public statements in the presence of the team about the accomplishments of individual athletes. He believed that recognition was an essential reward, a motivator, and a part of the fun of sports. He advised

> While excessive use of physical rewards in training may be a doubtful practice, they can be used as a symbol of recognition of a job well done, and can serve as motivators. An example is the reward of a few jelly beans given to the swimmer doing his best set of repeats or achieving some goal set by the coach. Once a season, at Indiana University, we have what we call "jelly bean day." Any swimmer achieving a given time in an over distance time trial (880 yards) receives one pound of jelly beans. The times are 9:10 for 880 freestyle, 10:20 for butterfly, and 11:30 for breaststroke. The writer feels it is an important part of the boys' training schedule to do some over distance, swimming hard. It is easier to motivate them and they swim faster for one pound of jelly beans and the success it symbolizes than they would if the coach were merely to assign an 880-yard swim in practice without the formality of "jelly bean day." College boys, and this coach, at least, are just grown-up children, and are motivated by the same means as are age-group swimmers. Coaches who forget this fact and are nothing but "cold turkey" at practice are missing a lot of enjoyment for themselves and their swimmers. (1968, p. 342)

In a similar vein, Counsilman recognized good grades and provided a free dinner each semester to each swimmer who made a 3.0 grade point average or better. For those earning below that he imposed a one dollar fine.

7. Self-Esteem

Doc's one dollar fine was purposefully trivial for he had learned from his old coach in St. Louis that the need for self-esteem is important to everyone. He believed it could be achieved by all despite the fact that not every swimmer and coach can be a winner. Counsilman (1968) knew and said that "With intelligent, hard work, each can achieve the best that is within him or within his team, and this is the standard he will be measured by, both by other persons and himself. 'My self-image is more important to me/Than what my neighbor's opinion might be' " (p. ix).

The guidelines Doc used to build self-esteem in his athletes were variations of the principles advocated by Dale Carnegie in his book *How to Win Friends and Influence People*. The coach chose them primarily as guides to protect a person's self-esteem.

1. Make every swimmer, assistant coach, and manager on your team feel he is an important, contributing member. By giving praise and recognition when it is warranted, you will convey that message.
2. Be genuinely interested in the other person, know his name, his interests, and his needs.
3. Before you talk about a swimmer's mistakes, allow him to rationalize them by sharing the blame with him: "John, you went out too hard in that race, and that was my fault for not telling you to control the first hundred."
4. Never prove another person wrong. Don't say to an assistant coach, "I told you we shouldn't have swum Jim on the relay. Now we've lost the meet just because you insisted he would do better than Harry." (Counsilman, 1977, pp. 256-257)

Counsilman, like every coach, wanted champions on his teams, but he did not make that a specific goal. Champions emerged in part because he enhanced the self-esteem of all of his athletes. As Doc said:

Nowhere in this discussion have I mentioned the development of champions as a goal. Only a fraction of one percent of your swimmers will ever swim in the Olympic Games, but all who participate in your program can gain the benefits of competitive swimming.

It happens too often that a coach is guilty of concentrating his efforts, attention, and hopes on only a few of his team members, at the cost of ignoring the others. This practice becomes so obvious to all who are involved: to those who are on the receiving end, the pressure becomes too great; to those who are neglected, the frustration becomes demoralizing.

The philosophy of a coach should contain room for developing the abilities of all the participants, not only those few who have proven their talents. You do not have to sacrifice the rest of the team to develop the exceptional few. Don't let yourself get caught in the trap illustrated by the remark of one swimmer's parent, "In a race there is one winner; he's the champ, the rest are chumps." Develop a state of mind that will concern itself with everyone on the team. If you do this you will have more than your share of champions, and fewer of these champions will have a distorted idea of their own importance. Teach the swimmers to respect one another by your own example. (Counsilman, 1977, pp. 258-259)

8. Challenge

Athletes especially welcome challenges and enjoy testing themselves and facing up to new experiences. A coach will receive positive responses from the athletes when the program is dynamic and innovative and when new challenges are placed before them. Doc was one for initiating new methods and techniques, for gambling and taking chances on new theories. His athletes took the stress positively because he involved them in the development decision and challenge of trying new methods. If a new method worked, the special thrill belonged to everyone; if not, they all went back to the drawing board and started over again. And as an added gain, it was never boring.

Honesty, truthfulness, integrity, sincerity, good humor, and a strong positive attitude filled in and reinforced the eight basic needs that formed the basis of Counsilman's coaching philosophy. That philosophy gave him direction and the wisdom to coach like few others.

Knowing the Job

Counsilman's philosophy of coaching didn't stop with philosophizing, however. He became the world's best coach in swimming because he had a clear vision of how to *apply* that philosophy. In his own dry words, a good swimming coach "is a good organizer who manipulates the swimmers' environment in order to motivate him highly to train hard and make the necessary sacrifices required to be a great swimmer" (1977, p. 268). Doc understood fully the sacrifices needed to achieve greatness, noting, " 'You've got to sacrifice a lot to be a good swimmer . . . it's not like football where you work out three or four months a year. The swimmers are working out actually 11 months a year. And they usually can't have summer jobs because they train too hard during summertime' " (Cecil, 1978).

The dullness of swimming workouts, plowing endlessly through the water, half sightless and soundless, is an environmental hazard that Doc worked hard to overcome. He attacked dullness on every front. Partly he used foolishness and horseplay to make the poolside time fun. Sometimes he wore costumes, made funny noises on the microphone, or tossed rock and roll albums in the pool, allowing the swimmers to toss in his classical music albums in return. No matter, the music played. Workout time was also for moments of challenge and reward. And as Doc told his swimmers, "Each practice session can be a course of scientific discovery" ("Coaches Can Be Their Own Scientists," 1987, p. 4). Fun, excitement, and accomplishment permeated Indiana's Royer pool. To Doc's boys it was home, an environment that the coach created to minimize the boredom and drudgery of their sacrifices.

To improve his professional contributions, Counsilman literally dissected the job of coaching; he argued that a great swimming coach had to be astute and knowledgeable in three areas—psychology, conditioning, and mechanics. To be effective, one must know how to work with swimmers—people skills; one must know the conditioning process—physiological skills; and one must understand stroke techniques and body motion—technical skills.

Of these three roles, the psychologist-coach is the most important, according to Doc. However, in his time, Counsilman was also the preeminent specialist in conditioning and mechanics for swimming. As he knew, a failure to understand conditioning and mechanics is bound to undermine the strengths and effectiveness of coaching psychology:

A coach who understands only psychology and nothing of the other two areas has already destroyed some of the psychological preparation of his swimmers, for they realize they are being coached by an incomplete coach who, as they say, "can psych us up for the race but doesn't know anything about stroke mechanics or training." A coach who has knowledge in all three areas has the ability to build confidence—a much-needed trait in psychological preparation. (1977, p. 269)

Counsilman knew that to build confidence in others you must first win their confidence. He reasoned that if his swimmers had confidence in him and the program, they would have the confidence to perform near their peak in big meet competition. "Athletes look to their coach for counsel and to borrow strength" (Counsilman, 1977, p. 269). Confidence was the essence of mental preparation; it not only strengthened athletes for telling moments, but it provided an essential basis for leadership development.

Doc emphasized and followed seven procedures to build confidence and proper mental preparation in his athletes.

1. Set reasonable goals for athletes.
2. Use only positive statements in discussions.
3. Help the athlete rationalize and understand poor or disappointing performances.
4. Help the athlete plan intelligently for a race.
5. Be knowledgeable of the sport; for swimming, as noted, this required expertise in psychology, physiology, and mechanics.
6. Be strong-willed; don't waiver in your determination or lose yourself emotionally during the competition.
7. Don't convey the coach as indispensable—rather work to build self-reliance in the athlete. (1977, p. 271)

In addition, there was a toughness and strength of determination in Doc that exuded confidence. In 1979, about two-thirds of the way through his coaching career, he became at the age of 58 the oldest person at the time to swim the English Channel. As Charlie Hickcox, world record setter in five events (1967-1968), told me in 1990, "Doc's toughness is amazing, I could never do that—I hate cold water." Hobie Billingsley reacted similarly: " 'I thought he was nuts until he left for England and I thought, "Oh, my God, he's going to do it because it's his nature: He would die before he quit" ' " (Sutton, 1990, p. C-12).

Finally, Doc also built self-confidence in his athletes by showing he had confidence in them, as this report illustrates:

One year Michigan swimmers, almost always a distant second to IU in the Big Ten meet, came to Bloomington boasting how they were going to whip the Hoosiers. Knowing that was impossible, Counsilman had a blackboard in the pool area on which he wrote which Hoosier would swim which event.

Hobie Billingsley, recalls the moment: "These (Michigan) guys are all mouthing off how they're going to beat us, and he (Doc) put this sign up on the blackboard and said 'OK, here are the events. Just sign up for which ones you want to swim,' " Their guys came in and saw it and, boy, were they - - - -. . . . They never got over that." (Sutton, 1990, p. C-12)

In this instance, Doc showed both Michigan and his own swimmers his confidence in the team, and this helped build their self-confidence. He takes pride in the fact that as many of his swimmers set world records in his absence as in his presence. This ratio is a tribute to the self-reliance his program instilled in his athletes at IU.

One Little Regret

Hobie Billingsley recalls a day in 1960 when he and Doc stood on a mound of dirt where the school's new pool was under construction. Doc turned to Hobie and said: " 'You and I are going to build a dynasty right in that hole,' " and Hobie replied, " 'OK Doc, let's get with it' " (Sutton, 1990, p. C-12).

Their dynasty ended three decades later. On February 3, 1990, after IU beat OSU (71-33) in Doc's last home meet, his last team captain, Geoff Clippert, read from a plaque presented to Doc by his last team. It was officially "Doc Counsilman Day" in Bloomington, and Geoff read aloud to the audience of 800 people at Royer Pool:

"Dr. James Counsilman . . . The World's Greatest Swimming Coach . . . Father of Swimming . . .

"We thank you for making the swimming world what it is today . . . you have established yourself as swimming's foremost authority and your innovative coaching techniques helped build a swimming empire at Indiana University that has been recognized worldwide. Your swimmers have not only recognized you as a coach but as a father figure, and your impact on our lives will always be felt and never forgotten." (Hammel, 1990)

Later talking to friends and reporters, Doc admitted to one minor regret: " 'When we came into this pool (1961) I counted the places on the wall for pictures and I said to Hobie, "There are 24 spots. Before I quit, we're going to fill them up." ' " At Royer Pool the walls are reserved for team pictures of the Big Ten champions. His six NCAA champions' portraits are hung in the IU campus Assembly Hall. " 'Look what's left. One spot. I didn't quite make the goal of twenty-four.' " He hung his head and took a long pause, then lifting his eyes went on. " 'We missed it by one.' " His words worried his friends who feared he might be letting that empty space really bother him, but true to his philosophy and positive character, he beamed a smile and said, " 'Of course, you know what the swimmers are saying, "23 is better than 22" ' " (cited in Issacson, 1990, p. 3-10).

Counsilman dominated his sport like no other coach, and did so for a quarter of a century largely because he pursued his own philosophy of meeting the hierarchy of needs in others. He provided his athletes with love and affection, security, status, achievement, group instinct, recognition, self-esteem, and challenge, and met his own needs in return.

On Saturday, September 15, 1990, I wangled my way into a Bloomington retirement dinner banquet for Doc attended by hundreds of his athletes and friends. The collection of world renowned athletes was enough to cause a mind warp, and the mutual respect, care, and love displayed was a priceless memory even for an outsider. Throughout the evening and on through a special brunch at Doc and Marge's home the next day, one great name after another gave back to Doc reminders of the timeless wisdom that he had given each of them—that life is a process, not an outcome. Their all being together again for that brief time was such a joy; it meant something noble, and, sadly, may never happen again.

James "Doc" Counsilman, scientist-coach and philosopher extraordinaire, wanted to be appreciated by his own athletes the way he had appreciated his own old coach, Ernie Vornbrock. According to the record, and from what I personally witnessed that unforgettable mid-September weekend, he succeeded.

Doc Counsilman's Head Coaching Record

Year	Record	Big Ten	NCAA
1958	5-2-0	6th	12th
1959	6-2-0	2nd	3rd
1960	5-0-0	2nd	3rd
1961	8-0-0	1st	—
1962	9-0-0	1st	—
1963	10-0-0	1st	—
1964	9-0-0	1st	2nd
1965	7-1-0	1st	2nd
1966	8-1-0	1st	2nd
1967	9-0-0	1st	3rd
1968	10-0-0	1st	1st
1969	11-0-0	1st	1st
1970	12-0-0	1st	1st
1971	14-0-0	1st	1st
1972	13-0-0	1st	1st
1973	14-0-0	1st	1st
1974	12-0-0	1st	2nd
1975	12-0-0	1st	2nd
1976	9-0-0	1st	4th
1977	9-0-0	1st	4th
1978	7-0-0	1st	9th
1979	9-3-1	1st	7th
1980	10-2-0	1st	9th
1981	12-0-0	2nd	14th
1982	9-1-0	2nd	16th
1983	8-3-0	1st	24th
1984	6-3-0	1st	18th
1985	10-2-0	1st	31st
1986	3-3-0	2nd	24th
1987	3-4-0	3rd	28th
1988	7-2-0	3rd	16th
1989	7-4-0	4th	12th
1990	5-4-0	—	—
Totals	288-37-1		

(Cont.)

Doc Counsilman's Head Coaching Record (Continued)

* Won Big Ten breaststroke title at Ohio State in 1946 and 1947.
* Coached IU to 20 consecutive Big Ten championships beginning in 1961, and 23 championships overall.
* Coached IU to six consecutive NCAA championships, 1968-1973.
* Coached 140 consecutive dual-meet victories from 1966-1979.
* Coached U.S. Olympic team in 1964 and 1976.
* Coached 74 IU swimmers to individual national championships.
* Wrote *The Science of Swimming*, still in print after 20 years and published in 20 languages.
* Inducted into the International Swimming and Diving Hall of Fame in 1976.
* At age 58 became the oldest person at that time to swim the English Channel in 1979.
* Designed IU Natatorium at Indianapolis, site of the 1990 NCAA meet.

"If IU had not had Doc it wouldn't have had a swimming program. They might as well have closed the pool," says Charles Hickcox, an ex-Hoosier in the International Swimming and Diving Hall of Fame.

Mark Spitz says he likely would not have won seven gold medals at the 1972 Olympics without Doc Counsilman's coaching.

Chet Jastremski once held four world breaststroke records and became a Pan American Games gold medalist while swimming under Counsilman at IU.

Chapter 5

Brutus Hamilton:
Life and Athletics
in Perspective

1952

The 14-member Olympic Committee was scheduled to meet on Saturday, February 2, at Chicago's Hotel LaSalle before announcing their selection, but on the preceding Thursday, the *New York Herald Tribune* had scooped them: "Brutus Hamilton Slated to Be Named Coach of U.S. Olympic Trackmen Saturday." The news leak came from a most reliable source, none other than the committee chairman, Pincus Sober, who confessed, " 'Brutus is one of a dozen

Brutus at Edwards Stadium timing his runners doing repeats on the track.

99

eligibles our committee submitted to the executive board . . . but it's an open secret isn't it, that the country wants Brutus as head coach. He's my personal choice' '' (p. 23). So certain was the decision that on Friday, February 1, Arthur Daley wrote the following in a feature article in the *New York Times*:

> The selection of Brutus Hamilton of the University of California as head coach of the Olympic track and field team is perfection itself. . . .
>
> For some unknown reason Hamilton has not received all the recognition he deserves as a track mentor, mainly because he never has been a publicity hound, hungry for headlines. Few men in the nation can match his record in the number of standout performers he has developed in virtually every event on the program. Brutus prefers to work along in his quiet, good humored way letting his actions speak for themselves. For Brutus is an honorable man. He's also a most versatile one.

Honor and versatility were two primary reasons "the country" wanted, and the committee selected, Brutus in 1952 as the head coach. His temperament and coaching philosophy were two other reasons. The tension and excitement that builds in every Olympic year is enough to test the mettle of any designated coach, but 1952, above all other years, was unique, and a unique man was needed.

Two wars were raging, one cold and one hot, each complementing and reinforcing the other. The Korean Conflict was in full swing, and the nations of the world anxiously watched the clash of "Red Armies" against the U.S. led forces. The Olympics scheduled for that summer in Helsinki promised little in the way of relief in world tensions, for they marked the first appearance in the history of the Games of Soviet participants. The first head-to-head competition of Soviets against Americans in track and field was hype enough for any sports enthusiast. Approaches to life and ideology were at stake, as well as honor and athletic performance. The Games became yet another test of communism versus capitalism. Which side would prevail? What incidents might occur? How would the participants accept winning or losing? Soviets had only recently shocked the world with their own successful testing of the A-Bomb, and the testing of the H-Bomb was imminent. No one could deny the heavy atmosphere of the Cold War and the possibility that minor errors could easily mushroom into major diplomatic catastrophes or worse. Curley Grieve (1952), sports editor for the *San Francisco Examiner*, conveyed the tenor of the times shortly after Hamilton's appointment:

> As the Communists seldom make a move without a motive, and sublimate even sports to the interests of State, most neutral observers believe that the Soviet sees in the Olympic Games an opportunity for rich propaganda. Otherwise, it would not be a party to a spectacle of such dimensions.
>
> Thus, some say, ugly little situations may arise which will call for diplomatic or perhaps forceful handling. If that happens, Coach Hamilton will be spotlighted. For a period of two weeks Hamilton may be our most important ambassador on any front, including those of Moscow and London. In fact, the State Department may hide advisors in Brutus's corner, just in case.
>
> What is his reaction at the present time to this touchy little matter?
>
> "I hope" he [Hamilton] says, "that the Olympic Games will be a clean, fresh breeze in the international atmosphere." And he adds: "I expect no troublesome situations to arise.
>
> If an American defeats a Russian, he'll pat the Soviet athlete on the back and with a modesty so inherent in Americans say, 'I was just lucky.'
>
> If a Russian defeats an American, I'm sure the Yank will shake the victor's hand and congratulate him. It is a natural reaction with us.
>
> The Olympic Games are for the glory of sport and honor of country and every athlete takes an oath to keep them that way. I am not worried at all about complications." (p. 1)

Others in the media pressed the hype in other ways. The *New York-Journal American* on February 5 (1952, p. 21), ran a United Press story typical of newspapers throughout the U.S. Entitled "Russia Big Threat," the article began "Russia was listed today as a major threat to the United States domination of track and field events in the Olympic games." Buried below in the article was Brutus's more cautious assessment: the Russians " 'have a pretty good all-around team' " (p. 21). The Olympic Committee recognized that Brutus was the right man to temper the excesses of the press and to instill a spirit of mutual respect at the Games, for the assignment of head coach was as much a mission of diplomacy as of coaching.

Olympic and Diplomatic Background

Brutus's credentials as an international sports diplomat were and remain unrivaled. He had been to every Olympic Games since 1920, where as a competitor at Antwerp in the decathlon he finished second, losing the gold medal by a mere four points. In 1924, he competed again in the decathlon, this time finishing tenth largely due to an injury. His keen sense of the Olympic spirit is reflected in his 1924 letter from Paris to his parents. Overcoming disappointment, he added perspective to those games refreshingly portrayed in the popular 1980s movie *Chariots of Fire*:

> "The track and field meet of the Eighth Olympiad is over. I have seen many things here which will linger in my memory forever. I have seen a small, lovable, 17-year-old high school boy, so homesick for his native California that he could hardly keep back the tears, crowned with the laurel wreath of victory in the pole vault. I have seen a 29-year-old sprinter come through and win his last Olympic start in one of the greatest comebacks ever staged, Jack Scholz of Missouri. I have seen a Scotch Presbyterian minister win the 400-meter race in world's record time. I have seen a 22-year-old boy weighing only 182 pounds, crowned victor in the shot-put and discus throw, although he was the smallest man in either competition. I have seen a man weighing 202 pounds vault 12 feet, 6 inches, and high jump 6 feet 4 inches. I have seen the great Paavo Nurmi, who prays two hours before each race; have seen him win four Olympic victories and earn the title of the greatest runner of all history. I have seen Willie Ritola win two races in world's record time and then take second to Nurmi in three other races. I have seen an old man lead his rivals over the long marathon course by five minutes, trot to the tape, walk to the stand to kiss his proud mother and then jog off the track as if he had only walked a mile. Well might Finland be proud of her sons. No wonder then that they all stood and sang their national anthem at the close of the games. In more ways than one, it was a Finnish victory." (Baack, 1975, p. 11)

In tense and difficult moments, the instincts for doing right are so very important. And, as incidents from his international coaching career illustrate, Brutus had positive instincts, anchored on a bedrock of good will. In the 1932 Games in Los Angeles, Brutus served as the U.S. Olympic Decathlon Coach. Jim Bausch, who had trained under Brutus at Kansas, was not expected to win the decathlon, but on the second day he cleared 13 feet in the pole vault. Several excited officials paged Brutus, who was in the stands, and implored him to tell Jim what to do. The confident Brutus replied, " 'I don't have to tell him anything, he knows what to do' " (Baack, 1975, p. 12). Bausch went on to win the gold medal. Brutus's quiet confidence no doubt helped.

In Berlin four years later, Brutus was again the decathlon coach of the U.S. Squad. Archie Williams, Brutus's own champion 400-meter runner from the University of California came to the starting line. Williams, like famed teammate Jesse Owens, found no easy arena as a Black athlete at the 1936 games, Hitler's so-called "Showpiece of Aryan Superiority." Though he had led throughout the 400-meter race, Williams's lead faded in the home stretch and the tension bore down on Hamilton. He began running vicariously in the stands. In the final seconds everyone stood as the race closed to the finish. In his exhausted excitement Brutus lurched and unintentionally kicked a German lady squarely in the ankle. Unable to apologize in German himself, he nevertheless effectively begged her forgiveness with hands clasped to his cheeks. She knew instantly, as did all who knew him, that his regret was sincere; and Brutus quickly found assistance to translate his apologies and explain his misconduct. And Brutus's joy at Archie's first-place finish was so radiant it affected her as well as others surrounding them (personal communication, 1965).

In 1949, Brutus traveled to Scandinavia as coach of the U.S. Amateur Athletic Union (AAU) team and was caught by a surprise request at a large postmeet dinner hosted by amateur athletic leaders from throughout Scandinavia, nearly all of whom could speak English:

> "All of a sudden the chairman begged for silence and when he secured it he said, 'I should like to call upon Mr. Hamilton, the coach of the winning team, to give us a toast.' This took me completely by surprise. I rose to my feet, not knowing what in the world to say, and all of a sudden there came to my mind

a toast which Jack London gave in 1903 to a group of publishers in New York. It goes like this: 'Here's to the four cardinal sins of man—stealing, lying, swearing and drinking. When you steal, steal away from dull companions; when you lie, lie to protect a lovely lady; when you swear, swear by your country; and when you drink, drink with me.' I then asked them all to drink with me to good sportsmanship and better understanding among all the peoples of the world. The toast went over big. I was asked to repeat it and many wrote it down. When I again visited Sweden and Norway following the Olympic Games of 1952, I was remembered not as an Olympic Coach or as the coach of the United States team in 1949, but as the man who introduced Jack London's toast to Scandinavia. I tell you this not to show that I am a clever person for, after all, it was Jack London who was clever, not me, but rather to show that, like the song says, little things can mean a lot on these tours." (Baack, 1975, pp. 95-96)

Brutus's Perspectives on the '52 Games

The outcome of the 1952 competition in track and field surprised even the most ambitious American supporters. Never before or since have the American men so thoroughly dominated the events (22 at Helsinki). Brutus's personal account of the Games gave his perspective as head coach.

Writing from London, August 1952 he said:

"The Games are history now; a magnificent chapter as far as the performances of our own boys are concerned. They were majestic, and almost to a man they did as well or better than ever before. Further than that, and even more important, their conduct was exemplary; humble but proud in victory, gracious in defeat. I know that you there at the office, and the alumni, even some who have written me such scorching letters about their end-zone seats, will give me much more credit than I merit for these performances. There is no false modesty about me, but I should know myself for a louse if I accepted a low bow for something for which I deserve only the slightest nod. The fathers who conceived and the mothers who bore and reared these fine boys deserve the bow for their splendid characters and exemplary behavior. The high school and college coaches who coached them so wisely and well for the final tryouts deserve the bow for their performances. To the credit of my assistants (who worked like dogs) and to myself let it be said that we did not interfere with the normal progress of the boys. For that, a slight nod only please.

"The gist of my talks with the boys can be reduced to just a few simple words,

" 'Honor yourselves, your country and your opponents with your very best performances and with your very best behavior. I'm certain you shall, for you are already well coached and your parents have already taught you right from wrong. You are a grand group of young men and we coaches expect this to prove the easiest coaching job of our lives.' It proved to be so; so again I repeat, don't give me undue credit." (Baack, 1975, p. 73)

From Brutus's accounts of the 1952 Games, one would hardly have known the stakes were high. He valued winning greatly, but preferred to emphasize the glory and human drama of participation. Indeed he was an eloquent sentimentalist, and for him the glory of the Games was best revealed in little things:

"If I were to choose one word to describe the Helsinki Games, that word would be 'graciousness.' The graciousness and kindness of the Finns toward all visitors. The graciousness of the competitors for each other; of the victors toward the vanquished; of the vanquished toward the victors. I shall long remember the graciousness of the girls who had charge of our dining hall; how they accepted the long hours, fed the hungry boys, but still kept sweet after a fourteen-hour day. Their happy smiles as they leaned forward and asked, 'More meat?' 'Porridge please?' 'More milk?' Their gracious 'thank you' as they served you. It's hardly possible that they shall remember the old weary man with glasses who kept coming back for more black coffee, but I shall never forget them. . . .

"Nor shall I forget Josey Bartel (Luxembourg) and Bob McMillan (USA) in the 1500 meters. Running the race of his life Bob almost caught Bartel at the tape. Bartel was completely overcome with sheer joy and pride and cried all during the victory ceremony. He was still overcome with emotion when I met him and Bob at the entrance to the dressing room some moments later. He threw his arms around me and said (in perfect English), 'Oh, Coach! My little country! I'm so proud for my little country! Our first Olympic medal ever—and it's *gold!*' Happy countrymen whisked him away. I looked at Bob. He, too, had lumps in his throat. 'I'm almost glad I lost to the little guy,' he said. 'He's so happy and proud.' And I thought the old Baron de Courbertin would have liked that—'For the glory of sport and the love of country.' " (Baack, 1975, pp. 75-76)

After the 1952 triumph in Helsinki, Brutus was showered with honors, including induction into the Missouri Sport Hall of Fame. There he was named Missouri's greatest amateur athlete ever. His mother, according to Brutus, provided an especially interesting and good-humored commentary on all the fuss:

"There is a moral to all of this," she twinkled. "It goes to prove that one should move away from his home community. Then, after 30 years, his friends will forget his many faults, his mischievous escapades and his general orneriness and remember only his virtues. I would write the selection committee, but I wouldn't know whether to congratulate them on their forgetfulness or their forgiveness." Brutus added "Not much danger of any of the Hamilton boys getting fat-headed or puffed up with such a mother." (Baack, 1975, p. 15)

A Philosophy of Perspective

Few barriers to athletic performance have captured the attention of the world like the four-minute mile. For decades leading up to 1954, coaches, athletes, and sportswriters had argued on its possibility. Just days before Roger Bannister carved a permanent niche for himself in sports history by running 3:59.4 at Oxford on May 6, 1954, Brutus published an article predicting the barrier's fall (Hamilton, 1954). Here are some excerpts:

Everybody talks about the four-minute mile and quite a few people are doing something about it. This Everest of the track world may soon be surmounted. When a runner achieves athletic immortality by finally accomplishing this goal, his name alone will be written in the record books, but, like the scaling of Everest, his achievement should be considered a team effort. Hillary and Tensing are the only ones who will be remembered for the Everest climb, but there are many others without whom their success would not have been possible.

Likewise, the four-minute miler should glance back over the years and pay tribute to those runners, coaches, and scientists who have made his achievement possible. He should look back to W.G. George and Alfred Shrubb, the great English runners of the latter part of the 19th century; to Nurmi who made running a ruthless and exacting science . . .

Zatopek Opens a New Vista. The eventual four-flat miler should make an especially low bow to Emil Zatopek of Czechoslovakia, the greatest long-distance runner of all time. Zatopek's work schedule, which he has given freely to all who ask for it, has caused a minor revolution in the conditioning of runners. . . .

Four-Flat Mile Within Reach. There was a time not long ago when most track experts thought the four-minute mile was beyond human capacity. It was pointed out that W.G. George, the English runner, had made a mark of 4:12-3/4 in the early 80's. Fifty years later only two seconds had been lopped off from George's time. Then came a new crop of runners and a new theory of distance running, culminating in the present 4:01-4/10 set in 1943 by Gundar Haag, of Sweden.

Who Will Be the First? Who will be the first to accomplish the four-minute mile? At the moment it would seem that Santee is the best prospect, but one can never be certain. . . .

It may be one of the fine English runners, of whom Bannister seems to be the outstanding hope. Bannister is a medical student at Oxford and prepares himself carefully for every race. . . .

Why Men Like To Run. People may wonder why young men like to run distance races. What fun is it? Why all that hard, exhausting work? Where does it get you? Where's the good of it? It is one of the strange ironies of this strange life that those who work the hardest, who subject themselves to the strictest discipline, who give up certain pleasurable things in order to achieve a goal, are the happiest men. When you see 20 or 30 men line up for a distance race in some meet, don't pity them, don't feel sorry for them. Better envy them instead. You are probably looking at the 20 or 30 best "bon vivants" in the world. They are completely and joyously happy in their simple tastes, their strong and well-conditioned bodies, and with the thrill of whole-some competition before them. These are the days of their youth when you can run without weariness; these are their buoyant, golden days, and they are running because they love it. Their lives are fuller because of this competition and their memories will be far richer. *That's why men love to run. There is something clean and noble about it.* [italics added]

Sport to Brutus was an important extension of humanity, and the best of athletic competition, he felt, was in the ideal of competing for the joy of it. He coached his runners to run for the love of it; to see something clean and noble in it; and to appreciate their personal accomplishments in proper perspective.

Brutus's athletes were taught that progress was the result of personal and team efforts, and they recognized and appreciated that each generation stands on the shoulders of those preceding. In fact, Brutus's example and teachings were shoulders all his athletes stood on. Twenty-nine years after his marvelous triumph in the 400 meters at the Berlin games, Archie Williams stood before a large teary-eyed audience at a testimonial dinner honoring Brutus. He tried, as had several other speakers, to find the words to convey his appreciation to the coach for his influence on him. No one there will forget Archie's words: "When I face a difficult situation, I ask myself what would Coach do."

Like Archie and others I've asked myself the same question many times, but obviously there's no formula or model or clever code of conduct that Brutus had to give to others. And yet he had a knack for placing things in perspective that helped all, and his most repeated advice to "his boys" as he called us was "keep things in proper perspective." It was his philosophy of coaching.

Recalling my first race as a freshman (1959-1960), there were no long talks of tactics, pace, or strategy. Brutus simply said, "This is your first race for the University, make yourself proud of the association." You couldn't help feeling as if you were part of a noble enterprise with Brutus. Once, just before the mile run at the Big Meet (Stanford versus California), Brutus waved us over. Unlike my running mates, I was so nervous I felt like throwing up. Brutus said to us, "Don't underestimate your competitors, honor them with your best performances." It gave us focus and a simple objective—our best performance—and it worked, as his words of perspective so often did.

One of the things that impressed me most about Brutus was his ability to find the good in a situation—his knack for a noble perspective. I personally benefited from this because, although a modestly productive cross-country runner, I scored only a few points in track each spring season in the one-mile or two-mile runs. My insignificance didn't seem to register with Brutus though, because he didn't rank his boys by their points, and more than a few times he told me that I was one of his "secret weapons." Progress and competitiveness were important to him, but he didn't favor gifted athletes in pursuit of winning. Each athlete contributed positively to the team, as Brutus saw it, by working and progressing; each contributed to the competitive pressure up the pecking order of talent in an event. For example, although only three runners could normally score points in a race, the fifth-string miler put pressure on the fourth-string runner, and the fourth pressured the third, and so on up the ladder to the team's best miler.

Sometimes the subtle forces of competitive pressure even worked across events. No doubt, for example, our best high-jumper wondered occasionally if he were as good an athlete as our best pole-vaulter or high-hurdler. Brutus recognized this and demonstrated it one afternoon while "fine tuning" Olympians Jack Yerman (400 meters) and Jerry Siebert (800 meters). He instructed them both to run 660 yards, telling Jerry to set the pace for 440 yards, and Jack to take over from there. Jerry, a straight-A student in physics, was bewildered. " 'Coach what should I do?' " he asked. Brutus simply replied, " 'Don't let him pass you' " (Baack, 1975, p. 6).

Hamilton had the talent to see routinely the good in things and to add perspective positively, a knack undoubtedly acquired over many years. It had proved a liability to a younger Hamilton; like Woody Hayes, Brutus loved literature and history and he too majored in them in college. Earning Phi Beta Kappa honors and being a gifted writer, he considered graduate studies in history. As Baack (1975) reports, the chairman of the History Department at the University of Missouri advised Brutus against this plan: " 'In the first place you're a sentimentalist and an idealist. The historical papers you would write would be sentimental, probably even maudlin, and entirely unrelated to the facts' " (p. 15). Brutus was never unfactual, but the professor had a point.

Brutus giving instructions to Jack Yerman (left) and Jerry Siebert (right) for a special workout at Edwards track.

Jerry Siebert (left) and Jack Yerman (right) warm up with Brutus looking on.

Brutus's stories were typically sentimental. For example, in 1941 Brutus was sympathizing with Pitch Johnson, the new Stanford coach, whose team had just been walloped by Cal in the Big Meet. Brutus recalled for Pitch his first year at Cal. In 1933 Stanford beat Cal 95-36, and if it hadn't been for a couple of Stanford boys being hurt, the defeat might have been worse. Brutus also recalled that as he wandered wearily home, downcast and depressed, and flopped into his easy chair, his six-year-old daughter Jeanie crawled up on his lap and said, "Don't worry, daddy, the Stanford boys are Americans too." (One can't help but think that more than once, in 1952, Brutus also must have thought of this sentimental moment, drawing the perspective that Russians, after all, are people too.)

Few rivals possessed Brutus's knowledge of track and field, yet his success, and the success of his athletes, was not due to any special advantages of technical expertise. Indeed, by the time I first met him in 1959, he was 59, an old man from my 17-year-old perspective, and his "workouts" were just routine and pretty much the same ones he had used for decades. Nor was the intensity excessive. Word had it, for example, that the Stanford boys trained a lot harder than we did. In this regard, he stood entirely apart from Lombardi, Hayes, Wooden, Counsilman, and especially Cerutty.

Rather than drive his runners, Brutus typically gave each of us an assignment well within our reach. If we were capable of running faster or doing more repeats, we would, he reasoned. Rather than force us, Brutus's aim was to motivate us to want more work. Like Hayes and Counsilman, Brutus kept a careful eye on our personal circumstances, our academic demands and capabilities, and other factors of our lives. Above all else, he didn't want to impose stress on his athletes. He wanted hard work, yes, but in an atmosphere of joyful dedication and fun. He also endeavored to build within each runner a burning desire to go faster. He worked this strategy just at the time it was appropriate to back off and ease up the workouts.

For example, I recall Alan Gaylord, Cal's best distance runner in the early 1960s, puzzling over one of Brutus's workouts for him: 12 quarters at 70 seconds with our routine quarter-lap jog between each one. Alan wanted to run three miles under 14:00 the forthcoming Saturday. How was he going to do it by merely practicing "easy" 70-second pace quarters? Thanks to Brutus, Alan had not only the leg to do it, but a frustrated, pent-up urge to go faster—and he did.

Coach the Whole Person

There was always a sense of balance and proportion with Brutus. Winning was important, but not winning at all costs. The pursuit of winning should never come at the expense of values, and he viewed the university as a place where people came to improve themselves and to prepare for life's greater challenges and rewards. Although important, athletics was seen by him as only a part of the human growth process. Indeed, he argued that within the university environment, athletics should be subordinate to learning; athletics was to contribute but not to dominate the main purpose of the university—intellectual development. He routinely asked the boys about their academic progress, often in great detail. An example of Brutus's balanced perspective is given in this paragraph from a recruiting letter Don Bowden provided to me, dated July 29, 1954:

> There is not much I can add to what I told you when you last visited the campus. You know pretty well what kind of a coach I am, since we have visited together and since you heard me speak at your meeting there in San Jose. You know our facilities, our schedule, and you know the prestige of the University as an educational institution. There can be no degree more coveted than one earned here. I think you know, too, that we have a healthy attitude toward sports here at Berkeley. We want our boys to win; we want them to maximize their potentialities in sports, but *we don't want them doing so at the expense of the more serious phases of college life* [italics added]. Your principal purpose in going to college, of course, is to get an education in your field of study which will probably be medicine. If you can break the world's record in the half-mile, which seems quite likely to me, while doing this, well and good. The main thing, however, is to be graduated a capable, self-reliant young man which your parents and friends want you to be. I can assure you that we here in the Athletic Department will do everything possible to see that your goals are achieved.

Don Bowden chose Hamilton's program and became America's first sub-four-minute miler by running 3:58.6 at a meet at the University of the Pacific [Stockton, CA] on June 1, 1957. He graduated from Cal two years later, and, with the 1960 Olympics on the horizon, talked with Brutus about going for a world record in the

Brutus with Don Bowden, first American to break a 4-minute mile.

mile. Brutus told Don that he could make him faster, but that the sacrifices would be too great. A world record not worth it! Brutus saw it that way, and so did Don. As Don told me, "Keeping running a part rather than my whole life is why I ran for Brutus and went to the University of California in the first place" (personal communication, September, 1990).

I was extremely fortunate to be on the team, from 1959 to 1963, when the shadow of the great Don Bowden was still cast, and when men like Jack Yerman (gold medalist, 1960 Olympics), Jerry Siebert (two time Olympian, 1960 and 1964), Dave Maggard (Olympian, 1968), and many other outstanding men were on the team. As emphasized above, however, never did any "plugger" or "secret weapon" type like me feel unimportant to the team. Brutus was incapable of making anyone feel left out or second class. A personal best effort was acclaimed by Brutus with the same special attention as a new course or meet record. There was nothing rah-rah about Brutus's positive reinforcements; he let teammates know you counted and when you were at your best.

Fast or slow, good or bad, all the athletes knew Brutus was there to help—even when the costs were high. In 1958, an explosive Black shot-putter named Proverb Jacobs, who stood 6′5″, blew sky high at a meet when an official ruled one of his throws a foul. The previous fall, Proverb had been on the football squad, but in a moment of temper, he busted one of his teammates on the chin, knocking him out cold; the coach, Pete Elliott, booted him off the team. Although Proverb almost ate the track official alive, he quickly grasped the seriousness of his outburst and retreated to the shot-putter's bench. Reporters asked Brutus after the meet, Would Jacobs get the boot again? The great basketball coach Pete Newell, who was Athletic Director at the time, tells us Brutus's reply: " 'Why of course not. . . . A coach's job is to help his boys, help them in every way possible. How could I help this boy if he is not on the squad?' " (Scott, 1965, p. 5)

Brutus's belief in Proverb paid off; Proverb went on to a successful, happy, productive life. When a reporter for the *Berkeley Daily Gazette* asked him in 1965 to reflect on the incident, Proverb responded, " 'Why I could talk all day about Brutus. I really don't know where I would be today if it weren't for him. I don't think that Berkeley people realize what a truly great person he is. I know it now that I've had time to reflect back on his philosophy and the way he deals with every individual. You have to be on his track squad to get the feel of this wonderful man' " (Scott, 1965, p. 5).

And how did Brutus help Proverb with his temper problem?

"He never bawled me out," said Proverb. "He never sweet-talked me. Rather, there was just something about him that told me he cared about me. He was the first person who ever did. I knew he understood my problems. And, brother, I had them. I was really hurt when I was kicked off the football squad. I wanted to bust something again. But soon I had become so fond of Brutus that I couldn't do anything bad. I knew it would hurt him. I was going to bust that track official. But just then I thought of Brutus. It would have been like hitting him.

"I guess he taught me character by example. No matter what happened, Brutus never lost his poise. He always conducted himself like a gentleman. He always said the right things. I found myself wanting to be like him." (Scott, 1965, p. 5)

Lon Spurrier, who set the world record in the 880-yd in 1955, is credited with explicitly recognizing one of Brutus's consistent

virtues: He was always there to share the blame for poor performances, but never around to share the credit for great ones. When
Lon passed the 660 mark en route to the world record, he heard
Brutus yell, "Better than world record pace, keep going." Wanting
to share the joy of the moment with Brutus, he ran to find him near
the 660 mark, but Brutus had slipped away. Lon faced the press,
the yelling crowd, and his jubilant running mates and friends by
himself. The moment was his alone.

Brutus never hesitated, however, to take upon himself the blame
for a poor performance, as in this letter written on November 16,
1960 to Stanford coach Payton Jordon:

> Your generous suggestion to postpone for one year the award-
> ing of the Old Time Athletes Cross Country Trophy because
> of the illness of our captain, Alan Gaylord, is hereby refused.
> Your boys ran well; mine didn't. Your team deserved the win
> and it would be an injustice to them not to let their names be
> the first on this new and lovely trophy.
>
> It is by no means certain that we could have won the race even
> with Alan at his best. Judging from the way my other boys
> performed he probably wouldn't have been at his best in any
> case. Two of my boys, George Linn and Gordon Whitehead,
> were the only ones from California who performed up to
> capacity. This was no doubt due to the fact that both boys
> work out for the most part on their own; Whitehead on the
> basketball court and Linn on the grass at Hearst Field late in
> the evening long after his coach has gone home.
>
> Alan, like the rest of the squad, had the misfortune to work
> out under my guidance. Somehow I fouled up the work-outs
> after the San Jose meet for none of the boys were sharp. Even
> granting that Alan is an unusual runner and generally wins
> despite his coaching, it's still questionable whether he could
> have turned in his all-time best race yesterday. He would
> certainly have had to do this to beat Rich and John.
>
> In the event you still persist in postponing the award for one
> year, I have yet another ace in the hole. I was president of the
> Old Time Athletes Association at the time the award was
> approved. Acting upon the authority vested in me as president
> of that organization, I declare your suggestion unconstitutional
> and out-of-order. You are therefore ordered to have inscribed

upon the trophy these words, "Stanford—1960"; and if room permits, the names of your first five men. I hope this disposes of the matter.

And on avoiding the credit and putting a world record in perspective, his letter (dated March 28, 1955) to Mr. and Mrs. Spurrier read

You are aware by now, of course, that your son Lonnie ran himself into athletic immortality last Saturday afternoon by breaking the world's record in the 880-yard run. The significance of this achievement has not even become apparent to Lonnie. It came with such stunning suddenness that he scarcely realizes how very important it is. It will dawn upon him when he begins to get letters from track fans from all over the world, congratulating him on this achievement.

When one considers that the half-mile has been a regular event in track meets for the last 150 years and that thousands of men all over the world have competed in the race, one begins to realize just how important a world's record is in this event. It means that Lonnie has run the fastest half-mile ever achieved by a human being and that he not only broke the record but that he broke it by over a second. It is a great valedictory to a young man who has fought injuries and illness to come through with the greatest half-mile ever run. He may even go faster yet if he keeps well and if his Air Force duties give him a chance to train.

I really think the significant thing from your viewpoint is that Lonnie is the same wholesome, unspoiled young man that he was prior to the race. He has had an excellent attitude toward athletics and has *never let sports interfere with the more serious purposes of college life* [italics added], nor will he ever let success in sports get him out of balance with life in general. His attitude has been ideal and will continue to be so. He has stern stuff in him, a noble inheritance from you two good people, and his achievement in sports will be only one of the many reasons why you will be even more proud of what he accomplishes in his chosen profession later on.

It has been a source of great pride to me to work with Lonnie and it has been a source of great satisfaction to observe how he has developed as a student here and what a good influence he has been on this campus.

He was graduated in February a capable, self-reliant young man, which you would expect him to be. I thank you for sending him to the University of California and I join with you in pride of his achievements.

Brutus knew that great performances could be achieved during a collegian's years at school, as so many of his boys proved, but more frequently great performances and other achievements came after the college years. Brutus devoted himself to helping people prepare for the future beyond the 4 years of college life. To sacrifice the long perspective was unthinkable to Brutus. His concern was for the whole person, in the context of winning and losing, as he stated at a Marin Sports Injury Conference in 1962. No doubt his words caught many in the audience by surprise.

We are living in a victory-made, record-conscious time. There is a professional intensity creeping into interscholastic and intercollegiate sports comparable to the training of the professional ballet dancer. Some of this is good; some of it bad when it interferes with the more serious purposes of life; when it threatens to sow the seeds of moral decay into the lives of our young men and even into the lives of some of our institutions of higher education. Alumni and even administrators of some of our colleges want victory and some of them are not too particular how the material to assure those victories is brought into the institution, or what becomes of the young men after their competition is completed. "Yes, Victory is great but sometimes when it cannot be helped, Defeat also is great," sang Walt Whitman. *No victory is great when it is bought at the sacrifice of ideals: and no defeat is disgraceful as long as one does his best and follows the gleam of idealism.* [italics added]. . . .

There is no need here to expand upon the potential values of sport as an adjunct to the educational processes. I shall say only that all of these values lose significance if they are not accompanied by ideals. *When ideals are obscured in amateur sports, then comes the danger of an athletic injury to the character of the athlete* [italics added].

Brutus worried more about character than winning and cautioned the audience that athletics can actually do injury to one's character:

A boy begins to show promise his sophomore year in high school. He gets into a few games or meets. He sees his name in the paper, maybe even his picture. He improves his junior year, is a regular on the team and his scrapbook gets thick. His senior year he really blossoms out, makes all-state, sets new records, gets notices in all the papers and magazines. He's the most popular man in his student body; every child in the community knows him and tries to emulate him. His parents are proud of him and justly so. He's a good lad.

Colleges began to rush him in his junior year. They go all out in his senior year. He is invited to visit many campuses, some of them out of the state. He accepts as many invitations as time permits. He is shown a wonderful time. He meets the college coaches, talks to some of the athletes on each campus, is shown the athletic facilities, sees some shows, meets some co-eds and goes to a dance. He is a little bewildered by it all, but it's good fun and he has a wonderful time on each campus.

Coaches, alumni, and friends of each college drop by his hometown and talk to his folks. They are very skilled in their presentations. They are all good salesmen. This school offers a free ride, board, room, tuition, and some spending money. Another offers tuition and an easy job. Each school offers some kind of financial inducement under one guise or another. The parents listen and become more confused as the summer progresses. They finally leave it up to the boy, and he accepts the offer which seems best suited to his particular inclinations.

It's easy to see where a boy can suffer an athletic injury to his character in such a situation. From his junior year in high school he has been subjected to pressures and publicity. He has been led to believe that he can get something for nothing; that life is going to be all primroses merely because he can run or jump or throw or shoot baskets or evade tacklers. He must have good stuff inside to keep his wits about him. He is called upon at eighteen to make decisions which would challenge those much older and wiser. It is to the everlasting credit of our athletic youth that so many of them turn out well in spite of the temptations put in their way.

Further athletic injuries to the boy's character can result in college. If he has chosen a school where sports are emphasized out of proportion to their importance he will find life easy if he performs well on the team. He will be coddled, made over, given parties by avid alumni, and even handed under-the-table payment, if not in cash then in some kind of presents. He's embarrassed at first, but soon comes to accept these things as a matter of course. The moral fiber gradually weakens and by the time his intercollegiate competition is over he is a victim of the system, a slave to gross and violent tastes, standing at the crossroads of Destiny. He was yesterday's headlines; he will be tomorrow's trivia. Now comes the harsh test as he faces the cruel pace of this competitive world in what he considers routine, humdrum chores of business. He gets no headlines now; others who are younger are taking his place. Some former athletes make the adjustment rather quickly, others grope for several years and then make the adjustment, usually with the help of some good woman. Others, all too many, drift into middle age and resort to artificial stimulation to substitute for the intoxicating experiences they enjoyed in sports. Maybe sports were only partly to blame, but I believe no one would criticize a doctor who diagnosed these cases as an "athletic injury to character suffered in youth."

The athletic injury to the mind is perhaps a little more tangible. First, there is the bright lad in high school who has a high I.Q. and is capable of making grades sufficiently high to qualify for admission to any college. But he gets carried away by the publicity and hero worship he receives in high school due to his athletic attainments. His grades slump, he ignores the admonitions of his coach and counselors and is content to merely pass. He gets his diploma but is disgusted with himself to find that he can't qualify for any first-rate college. He goes through a bad period of depression.

We have a number of these boys at the University of California. They are the ones who woke up. Many of them went into the Army or worked for a couple of years after high school. Then they went to junior college and made up their grades. They do superior work at the University, but they don't go out for sports. They've had enough. A doctor might diagnose their case as "suffered an athletic injury to the mind in high school—fully recovered."

The sad cases though are the ones which involve the eager, bright lad who goes to college on some kind of an athletic grant and is eager to become an Engineer, Lawyer, Doctor, Teacher or Architect. He becomes a victim of the intensity of the athletic training program. He misses practice to work on problem sets or to write out a book report. The coach suggests that he may be in the wrong course. Maybe he should transfer to a course which is not so demanding on his time. He certainly can't miss any more practices or his grant may be terminated. The boy has little choice, so he submits to the coach's suggestion and gives up his planned career. He may succeed gloriously in this new field but always he will wonder if he didn't make a mistake. He will always consider that he suffered an athletic injury to his mind in college whether anyone else does or not. When the training for an intercollegiate team becomes so time consuming, so intense and so exhausting that it is no longer possible for the student in the sciences or professions to participate, then something is wrong. Someone, perhaps a great many, are suffering an athletic injury to the mind.

One can only speculate on the guidance his family and coaches gave Brutus to avoid such sports injuries in his youth in Missouri, but one thing is clear: Brutus never sacrificed his athletes for the purpose of winning. His philosophy of perspective forbade it. Where other coaches were hard-driving and demanded total concentration, effort, and commitment, Brutus asked his runners to run for the joy of it. As he said, running was "clean and noble."

Mind Over Matter

In his letter to David Maggard* shortly after Maggard landed his first school coaching post, Brutus wrote " 'Coaching track will always be rather a personal coach-athlete relationship and not a mimeographed affair, non-personalized like a computer machine. Some coaches know all the techniques except they forget to tell their boys to get there first. They become so form conscious that

---

*Maggard ranked among the world's top shot-putters in the late 1960s and eventually became the head cinder coach at Cal and subsequently the Athletic Director. In 1963, he traveled with Hamilton to the Far East to conduct track and field clinics.

they invariably forget to win. Form is, of course, important and essential but it should never stick out' " (Baack, 1975, p. 6).

Brutus asked his athletes, during the limited time they could devote to training and to competition, to give a maximum effort and enjoy their strivings. Shortly before his retirement he told *Oakland Tribune* columnist Ed Levitt (1965) that his main purpose as coach was

> "To create within the athletes an interest and enthusiasm for the events. . . . then direct that interest and enthusiasm along the lines of sound fundamentals, taught imaginatively, intelligently, purposefully and even inspirationally. It sounds rather easy and simple, but it isn't.

> "No matter how much a coach has read, studied or observed, there will come times when he must sense things beyond his experiences and intuitively apply a new approach.

> "Each individual is different, and it's hard to generalize about anything as evasive as a human being. Someone once asked a voice teacher what method he used in teaching his pupils to sing.

> " 'I have 25 students,' he said, 'and I have 25 different methods.' No coach has the time to make his teaching quite that personalized, but it would be good if we did.

> "I wish I could point out some easy road, some primrose path, up the road to athletic success. But after more than 30 years in coaching young men, I'm afraid I have nothing more romantic to suggest than purposeful, planned, imaginative, enthusiastic, and inspirational work.

> "And some of the work must be hard. It need not be unpleasant work, however. It can be joyous and it should be if the best results are to be obtained. And it must be sustained over a long period of time." (p. 51)

Brutus didn't subscribe to work that became grim. Human energy had to remain spirited to realize best efforts. As he told it,

> "The more I coached the more I became convinced that the mind, the will, the determination, the mental approach to competition are of the utmost importance. Yes, perhaps even more than the improvements in form and technique.

"All of us have seen men of average ability—who strive to be something other than average—succeed in athletics.

"We have seen it in other walks of life as well. We coaches don't understand it as yet. Nor am I certain the psychologists do. But this motivating power of the mind is a force we all reckon with and a power which all coaches, directly or indirectly, try to direct." (p. 51)

Little Things

One afternoon after a hard workout, Brutus and I were chatting about graduate school, and he was delighted I was planning to continue my studies. It was a beautiful sun-drenched day and our two shot-putters, Dave Maggard and Matt Baggett, were walking across the midfield of the track toward the weight room. Together they weighed well over 500 pounds, with not a trace of fat visible on either one. It was a magnificent sight, this white and black power-packed pair. As they slipped out of earshot, Brutus whispered to me, "Thank God the Lord made them peaceful men."

Brutus exemplified inner peace, and, although he once was honored as America's all-around greatest athlete, Brutus was never "macho." Like a brilliant, poetic teddy bear, I never heard him raise his voice. Perhaps it was his own powerful physical stature that stirred his interest and adoration of little things.

At our daily workouts, Brutus sat in the empty bleachers in Edwards Stadium surrounded by happy well-fed birds. But it was the squirrels he loved the most, and several times in my senior year he took me along with him to rendezvous with one of his favorites. He called it by a chirping sound, and I recall pondering the possibility he could actually talk to it.

When his daughter Jeanie was in junior high, she wrote a poem called "My Day." One of the lines read, "Although my Daddy's very fine, he's not president, so little things instead of big make up my day's events." Perhaps troubled and melancholy about retirement coming in a couple of years, or just suffering a little from old age, he wrote her in 1963 and reflected on her words.

"If I am remembered at all, it will be for 'little things.' None of the several contributions which I thought rather pertinent at the time will be remembered a week beyond my departure:

but some nonsense which I have concocted or been a party to may earn me a tiny little footnote in the history of my time. I am not complaining, just amused and a little sad at this realization.

"For example, on campus I shall be referred to, if at all, as 'the kindly old fellow who used to feed the birds and squirrels.' This began years ago, shortly after Snitzie died, and Mommie and I decided against getting another pet. I took what money we budgeted for a pet and spent it for the wildlife here at home and on the campus. It has brought me much happiness and one sad experience.

"One gets to know the squirrels as there are not many of them; two especially stand out in my mind. One was an old, old one when we first became acquainted. His teeth were gone, and he could no longer crack a nut. When I diagnosed his difficulty, I began to crack the nuts for him and feed him the morsels. He was most grateful and was always waiting for me each morning. One day I forgot the nuts, and it was too late to go back so I decided to walk quickly past our trysting place in the hope that he wouldn't recognize me. It was to no avail. He recognized me, all right, and the first thing I knew, he was running between my legs and forced me to a halt. He looked up at me with unbelievingly scolding eyes. I raced right on past my office to the grocery and hurried back with some nuts. He was waiting and forgave me. Eventually, of course, there was a day when he didn't show up. He had left this life and had gone to his reward.

"The other was a diminutive female and the dearest little wild thing I ever saw. She became so tame, she would run up my leg and go right into my pocket for a nut. When I sat down, she would hop up on my knee and nibble away at her goodies. Every once in a while she would stop and look up at me with adoring eyes. I'll swear there was love and gratitude in them. One day I noticed she was getting heavy with children. She seemed so proud of herself. 'Don't you think I'm very clever?' she seemed to say as she looked up at me from her perch on my knee. She started building her nest in the oak tree just above our meeting place.

"Then one Monday morning she wasn't at the accustomed place. I called, but she didn't come. I thought I heard a noise down by the creek. There she was, trying to pull her heavy little body toward me. She looked up at me with sad, pained and bewildered eyes and died there at my feet. There was a hole through her body and caked blood on her flanks. I damn near cried. I borrowed a spade from the gardener and buried her there by the creek bank where we had met so often. (I heard later that some thoughtless little boys had snuck on campus with a high-powered air rifle Sunday afternoon.) For months your sentimental daddy always got a wrench when he passed under the tree and glanced up at his little friend's unfinished nest. The winter storms have finally removed the nest *and time, the healer, has permitted me to get things in perspective* [italics added]. I shall remember my little friend as a bit of beauty which came into my life and made me, I hope, a better and more understanding man.

> 'If I should pass some summer night mothy and warm
> When the hedgehog skirts furtively over the lawn,
> One may say, "He strove that such innocent creatures
> should come to no harm.
> But he could do little for them and now he is gone." '

"There I go, making you sad again with the help of Thomas Hardy. I didn't mean to when I started to tell this episode. Forgive me. I merely wanted to expand a little upon your theme of 'little things.' " (Baack, 1975, pp. 117-119)

My favorite Brutus story is one that my children request of me repeatedly, and that I have told the runners I coach. Before telling it, I predict goosebumps by the end, and first-time listeners usually admit getting them. Brutus's dad had been a popular man, the county sheriff, an avid hunter, and an accomplished dog breeder and trainer. Brutus tells about his dad's last dog.

"There is a sad and tender story connected with the last dog he ever owned—'Zero.' 'Zero' showed up on the farm early one morning in 1938. He was a little [ragamuffin] pup terribly tired and woe-begone and hungry. Had probably escaped from a passing car but the owners never came back looking for him. I asked Dad why he named him 'Zero' and he said 'That's what he cost me—and that's about what the little rascal's worth.' But I know no amount of money could have bought him from Dad. They were inseparable. Everywhere Dad went there was little old Zero right behind him. When Dad would go to town Zero was right behind him in the old Buick. He would follow him around as he did his shopping, never going into a store but waiting patiently at the front door until Dad reappeared. Houses and stores were 'off-limits' to him, including our own, and he knew it.

"That's why Mama and the nurse who had come in to help her were surprised when there came a frantic scratching at the front door about 11 o'clock in the evening of February 5th, 1943. It was of course little Zero who wanted to get in to see his master who had been ill and in bed for a week. No one thought he was critically ill but the doctor had put him to bed as a precautionary move. So Mama relinquished a long standing rule and opened the door and let Zero in. He went immediately to Dad's room, jumped up on the bed, and began to lick Dad's face. Dad petted him and talked to him a few minutes while Zero snuggled down on Dad's shoulder. After a while Dad told him he'd have to go now so Zero gave his face a last lick and hopped down and went back outside. It turned out to be their last 'love-in'; for Dad's heart suddenly stopped shortly after dawn on the morning of the 6th; and they found little Zero dead in a bed he had improvised on the front porch just outside the window next to Dad's bed. He had dragged the old rug and the old rags from his dog house during the night and had made himself a comfortable bed there on the porch next to the window.

"It was of course just a strange coincidence. Scholars tell us that a dog is not capable of thinking or of really loving. But some of the neighbors who had observed the devotion between Dad and Zero were certain that Zero had died of a broken heart. And my mother, who still had sixteen years to live, was never certain to her dying day that there hadn't existed a special affinity between the two, a certain strange intuitive genius on the part of Zero (he died a young dog) which led to this sad and touching end." (Baack, 1975, pp. 119-120)

There is a magnificent stand of redwood trees along Strawberry Creek in Faculty Grove on the Berkeley campus. It was a favorite spot of Brutus's where he fed the squirrels for many years. Shortly after his death, the university renamed it Hamilton Grove, and had an engraved plaque placed on a large stone there to honor him for eternity. A reception preceded the naming ceremony, and after the reception the gathering left together to walk up the hill to the Grove. As the group reached the rise and entrance to the trees, the afternoon sun broke through a cloud, impairing everyone's vision. In fact, it momentarily stopped the group's movement. Then a little squirrel bounced out of the ferns onto the path. Seconds later there was not a dry eye in the throng, and more than a few, men and women, were openly crying. Hamilton was right. Olympian, Silver Medalist, America's greatest all-around athlete in the 1920s, international ambassador, the nation's greatest track and field coach, and other accolades paled as those who loved him recalled Hamilton—"the kindly old fellow who used to feed the birds and squirrels." And all were reminded of Brutus's "special affinity" for little things that leads to this happy and touching end.

Brutus Hamilton's Head Coaching Facts

Born	July 19, 1900 in Peculiar, Missouri
College	Graduated from the University of Missouri, where he was a second-team All-American in football, a basketball player, and 1920 and 1924 member of the U.S. Olympic track team (in 1920 he placed 2nd in decathlon)
Coaching	Westminster College, Missouri—1924-1929 University of Kansas—1929-1932 University of California—1933-1965

Famous Athletes

George Anderson	1935 IC4A* 100-m champion
Larry Anderson	1954 NCAA pole vault co-champion
Jim Bausch	1932 Olympic and world record holder in the decathlon
Bob Biles	1942 NCAA javelin champion
Marty Biles	1940 and 1941 NCAA javelin champion and AAU javelin champion 1948 U.S. Olympic team member
Don Bowden	1957, first American to break the 4-min mile (3:58.6), Stockton, CA 1957 NCAA 800-m champion and National Collegiate record holder (1:47.2)
Bob Clark	1934 and 1935 AAU decathlon champion 1936 Olympic decathlon silver medal winner and 6th in Olympic broad jump
Hal Davis	Four-time AAU and NCAA sprint champion and co-holder of 100-m and 100-yd world records
Gene Johnson	1962 USA-Polish high jump winner (7'1/2'')
Bob Kiesel	Three-time IC4A sprint champion 1932 Olympic 400-m relay gold medal winner
Leamon King	1950s co-holder of 100-yd (9.3) and 100-m (10.1) world records
Grover Klemmer	1941 400-m record holder and world record for 1600-m relay (3:09.2) and 3200-m relay (7:34.6) 1958 world record for 3200-m relay (7:20.9)
David Maggard	1968 U.S. Olympic team member in shot put

(Cont.)

Brutus Hamilton's Head Coaching Facts (Continued)

Tom Moore	1935 co-holder of 120-yd high hurdles world record
Roger Olsen	1962 NCAA champion in high jump (6'10'')
George Roseme	1952 NCAA javelin champion
Jerry Siebert	1960 and 1964 U.S. Olympic team member in 800 m
Guinn Smith	1941 NCAA pole vault champion
	1948 Olympic pole vault champion
Lon Spurrier	1955 world record holder for 880 yd (1:47.5)
Archie Williams	1936 Olympic 400-m champion and world record holder
Jack Yerman	1960 Olympic and world record 1600-m relay team
Honors	Phi Beta Kappa
	Olympic decathlon coach, 1932, 1936
	Head coach of USA team visiting Scandinavian countries, 1949
	Head U.S. Olympic track and field coach, Helsinki, 1952
	Head coach of USA team at Maccabean Games, Tel Aviv, 1953
	Special coaching mission for U.S. State Department to India, 1954
	Head coach of USA team to Soviet Union, 1965

*Intercollegiate Amateur Athletes of America Association.

Chapter 6

Percy Cerutty:
Australia's Eccentric
Genius of Running

They Said It First

In 1950 the material well-being of the average American surpassed that of citizens of the other advanced nations by margins unsurpassed in history. The effects of two world wars had strewn ruin throughout Europe and Asia, and despite rapid resurgence by some nations, the United States, with only six percent of the world's population in 1950, was producing nearly one-third of the world's total output. In category after category, from manufacturing and energy, to

Percy Cerutty demonstrates the galloping running style he developed.

transportation and housing, food, entertainment, and sports, Americans out-did all others. Winning wars, and most every other competition imaginable, had become the American Way. Americans were tops. Like no other, the post World War II decade was America's most dominant.

The pervasive impression of American strength and dominance was punctured, however, in 1957 when Russia launched Sputnik, the world's first orbital satellite, and again in 1958 when two odd characters from Australia arrived in the United States to challenge America's best milers to a series of races. Herb Elliott, barely 20 years old and already the decade's most famous Australian, and his eccentric 63-year-old coach, Percy Cerutty, launched their world tour on American shores, taking on all challengers. Their commentary on American life rivaled their sports heroics for news headlines.

"Overwhelmed Appalled Shocked" read one of the section headlines in the *Sports Illustrated* cover story on Elliott and his coach (Connery, 1958). The highly vocal Cerutty blasted away like a licensed critic; Americans, he sneered, " 'are overfed, live over luxuriously and are mostly fat and flabby.' " He found Los Angeles, where Elliott promptly set a new American record in the mile (Coliseum Relays, May 16th, time of 3:57.8)*, " 'hurrying, scurrying, mad, amazing . . . with churches like business offices, business offices like churches . . . and six-month old babies propped in front of television.' " Elliott was similarly appalled at " 'the pasty look of America's pampered children' " (p. 77) and was fearful that his own countrymen, threatened with rising prosperity, might go soft the same way. As Elliott (1960) promptly put to words,

> When I say that I'm glad I was born Australian, not American, I hope all my American friends will not be offended. But I believe in frankness. And it's a fact that the warm, soft, synthetic existence Americans lead poses a real doubt about their future. A people who so thoroughly mollycoddle themselves must steadily become weaker, physically and spiritually. The Americans are not the only people who are insulating themselves from their environment; the tendency exists even in my own country. I shudder to think what would happen to

---

*At the time it was the second fastest mile in history (after Derek Ibbotson's 3:57.2 world record).

some of these pampered people who have separated themselves from nature if suddenly they were thrown back into the
natural environment that God provides. How many would
survive? (p. 74)

Their barrage of criticism actually began on first landing in
Honolulu. Describing Americans at Waikiki beach, Elliott (1960)
used Cerutty's own words, "They were fat and they were flabby.
. . . Even the kids. I saw a boy of no more than eight whose muscle
tissue hung on him limply like pieces of sacking, the end result, I
was sure, of two generations of soft living. Unlike Australian
beachgoers many of the frequenters of Waikiki couldn't swim ten
yards to save themselves" (pp. 75-76).

In Los Angeles, Elliott and Cerutty had to lay in a supply of dried
fruit and walnuts; they complained they could get nothing but
" 'soft asparagus and puffy fish' " (Connery, 1958, p. 77). Cerutty
was shocked by public signs advising what to do in case of a heart
attack.

Prompted by Cerutty's philosophies, Elliott (1960) analyzed the
predicament of American men:

Few American men, once they leave college, bother about
physical exercise, in marked contrast to Australian men who
are sport conscious from cradle to grave. I was disturbed also
by the quantity of rye and bourbon that the Americans drink,
which must be symptomatic of their discontent. Now, I believe
that you can tell a tree by its fruits. And the fact that the
Americans in recent years have not produced many outstanding distance runners is directly attributable to their soft way
of life. They are not a hardy race of people, whereas the
Australians, Norwegians, Russians and English are. (p. 77)

As Elliott diagnosed the American sport scene, he concluded that:

On the whole, Americans are not suited temperamentally to
any race beyond the 880 yards.

In facilities, few nations can match America. No matter how
complete these facilities, though, they cannot offset the national
characteristics of softness and complacency. In some ways
America's outlook reminds me of those personal tendencies I
try to guard against. To reach that pinnacle of achievement
where you're accepted as a leader you must be tenacious and

determined. Once there, it's natural to relax and rest on your laurels. Having reached its pinnacle, as it were, America lacks the aggression and initiative of smaller countries, who love nothing better than succeeding occasionally in knocking her off her perch. The fact that America still produces overall the world's best sprinters, high-jumpers, pole-vaulters and shot-putters shows that her people are capable of explosive bursts of energy and enthusiasm, qualities that make their business-men so effective. But, patently, sprinters and field-games men do not have to train as gruelingly as middle-distance and distance runners. Twenty 100 or 200 yard bursts in a night may tire a sprinter; they don't wring his lungs out as a ten-mile run would. (p. 77)

In unsurpassed material comfort, America had gone soft according to Cerutty, and Elliott (1960) echoed his thoughts.

Money seemed to play far too important a part in the way of life. It appeared to me that the people were forgetting the simpler pleasures of exercise, family life and the observance of nature in their pursuit of material possessions. Western civilization seemed to be becoming decadent, and I wondered whether there could be any parallel here with the decay of the Roman civilization. (p. 77)

Aside from softness, perhaps nothing annoyed Percy more than a coach who failed to practice what he preached. While in Los Angeles, soon after Elliott ran the fastest mile ever recorded on American soil, they both attended an instructional clinic on track and field at UCLA. All of America's leading coaches were there along with their athletes who went through prescribed paces and demonstrations while the coaches lectured to the audience of nearly 2,000. Puffing their cigars and cigarettes, the American coaches glibly ordered their athletes around taking about 15 minutes each on the microphone system. When it was finally Cerutty's turn to speak, he was told he had two minutes. He didn't need three. According to Elliott (1960), his coach "electrified the arena" as he called "all the coaches 'a pack of pompous clowns' who had no right teaching students in that fashion" (p. 36). When he'd finished, the coaches were bristling with anger and embarrassment.

Between May 31 and June 21, Elliott extended his unbeaten record in the mile with four more victories in California. His June

6, Compton Invitational time of 3:58.1, and his June 21 American championship victory in 3:57.9 at Bakersfield gave him the third- and fourth-best mile times ever run (along with the second he had already set on May 16). Then the odd pair flew to England where, on July 26, Elliott won the Empire Games mile in 3:59. Indeed, Cerutty trained athletes who won all of the long-distance races, from the half-mile to the marathon, at the 1958 British Empire Games.

The clash the world clamored and waited impatiently for came in Dublin on August 6. Ron Delany, the cocky, carefree, bright, and exciting Irish Olympic gold medalist (1956) was racing on home turf. His only defeat ever in the mile had come at the Compton meet two months earlier against Elliott. All of Ireland, and not just a few Americans, wanted Delany to triumph, a just revenge against this strange new force from down under. As Elliott entered through the stadium gates, an old Irish lady darted in front of him and tauntingly purred, " 'And welcome to Dooblen, oi wish youse luck and you're a nice stamp of a bhoyo and no mistake. Sure it's a pity our Ronnie has to beat youse today' " (Elliott, 1960, p. 3).

Another arch-rival there was Merv Lincoln, the Australian great whom Elliott had battled successfully before, plus two other Cerutty protégés, Albert Thomas (three-mile world record holder) and Murray Halberg, who ran with a withered arm and a steely determination akin to Elliott's. Six outstanding local runners rounded out the field.

As the bell lap sounded, Elliott slipped past Lincoln and started his patented long burst for home. Moments later the roar of 20,000 Irish matched the excitement of the disbelieving timekeepers. Above the noise of the frantic crowd came this announcement: " 'Elliott first, 3:54.5, a new world record; Lincoln, second, 3:55.9; Delany, third, 3:57.5; Halberg, fourth, 3:57.5; Thomas, fifth, 3:58.6.' For the first time in history five men had run sub-four-minute miles in the same race" (Elliott, 1960, p. 6).

The very next evening, Cerutty also reveled in glory as Albert Thomas set a new world record in the two-mile run. Elliott, who had helped pace him, was second. Three weeks later in Gothenburg, Sweden, Elliott set another world record by running the 1500 meters in 3:36 (comparable to a 3:53 mile). Three more wins in Sweden, England, and Norway extended his unbeaten streak in the mile (and 1500 meters) before he quit his 1958 world tour to return home.

The accolades poured in from all over the world, even from America. "The Amazing Herb Elliott" read the *Sports Illustrated* cover (November 10, 1958). Printed next to a picture of "Cerutty's private hell dune"—an 80-foot long, 60-degree sloped sand dune—with Cerutty leading Elliott and nine others up it, the article read

> Herb Elliott is an amateur athlete, but his approach to running is strictly professional. Under the verbal lash of his flamboyant coach-conditioner, 63-year-old Percy Cerutty, Elliott has whipped himself into the most relentless running machine in the world. From his first bowlful of dry John Bull oats, bananas, raisins and nuts in the morning to his five more pages of H.G. Well's monumental (1,200 pages) *Outline of History* before lights out, Elliott leads the "Stotan" life of sacrifice and self-reliance that Cerutty preaches from the examples of Stoics and Spartans. The object is to burn the legs off every middle- and long-distance front-runner in the world. (Connery, p. 77)

Elliott and Cerutty had stunned the sporting world, but the new world records by Elliott and Thomas had an added effect in America. Those triumphs gave license, perhaps even credibility, to Elliott and Cerutty's criticisms of American values and lifestyles. "Americans are getting soft!" Old Cerutty and young Elliott said it first. By implication, should the world look to the United States for leadership? At least two odd characters from Australia doubted it.

A License to Talk

Percy's tactlessness, some would say impudence, in labeling Americans "soft" and American coaches "pompous clowns" was not contrived. Such mischief was natural with him. Like few others, he had absolute confidence in himself. He enjoyed showboating, clamored for headlines, and bore a reputation at home and abroad as a rude, irreverent anticonformist.

What drew people's attention to him was not his stature in the organized sports world, for even the many vibrant athletic associations in Australia shunned him. He stood entirely alone, unaffiliated except with his conscience and beliefs. What made his words sting was the grain of truth in them, and his personal example of human toughness and total dedication to mental and physical excellence. Those qualities were contrived; they didn't come naturally or easily to Cerutty.

Born in 1895, Cerutty grew up in a working-class suburb of Melbourne. He was a weak, sickly, and underprivileged child. When he was six years old, he contracted a case of double pneumonia that caused partial paralysis of his left lung. For years, heavy exercise and especially running caused severe discomfort. Nevertheless, his extraordinary willpower triumphed over his frail physique for a period, and between 1913 and 1918 he entered 36 races, mostly the mile, winning 10 (1 in 4:32). Ill health, however, prevented him from training for the Olympics in 1920. He suffered from chronic migraine headaches and was usually sick after races. When he quit running in his early twenties, his health continued to slide. By the time he was 43, he had suffered a nervous and physical breakdown requiring a six-month sick leave from his job as a telephone technician. At that nadir of his life, he had lost all faith in himself. He was unable to approach even routine tasks such as driving a car.

In the ensuing six months of enforced rest, Cerutty's contemplations evolved an entirely new approach to life, one he figured would either cure or kill him. To steady his nerves and regain his confidence, he reasoned he must learn to dive off the high tower at St. Kilda Baths. He started with a three-foot leap and slowly over the next two years worked his way to the top. As his confidence grew, he took up weight lifting, mountain climbing, and hiking, often testing his willpower by plunging into the icy Yarra River near his home. In short, he rejected the stultifying city environment that had emaciated him. In his focus on the regeneration process, he pored through all the great books on philosophy, religion, and physiology plus autobiographies and works of poetry. His creed became *strength through nature* as he learned that the more he coddled himself with human comforts, the sicklier and weaker he became.

He pursued the reverse of comfort, thrusting himself against pain. As he spit in pain's face, his strength grew, and in his pursuit of nature, his civilized imposed limitations fell away. At 48 he took up marathon running, and at 50 years of age he could break three hours, a new native Victorian record for the distance. Soon after, he became one of the first three Australians to run 100 miles in under 24 hours.

By his mid-fifties, Percy was ready to launch a new career. Though poor and unsupported, he became a freelance coach. It wasn't for the money. The runners paid him a little money for the food he provided, but he mostly received work from his athletes in exchange for his services. Material comforts remained foreign to Cerutty.

His weekend seashore training retreat at Portsea steadily attracted more and more athletes, although as many left prematurely as stayed for a full dose of Cerutty's regime. As the athletes came and went, rumors spread afar about Cerutty's hideaway in the sand dunes where men trained in new ways, lived on bizarre diets of mostly raw foods, slept in ragtag bunk house shacks, and ran barefooted all year round. Many rejected it, some swore by it, but all agreed that tough old Cerutty had earned a license to talk. Cerutty was a living triumph of the human spirit and will.

Gathering Stotans

A 17-year-old Herb Elliott first saw Cerutty in 1955 when Cerutty visited Elliott's school in Perth. Elliott (1960) described his original reaction to Cerutty, then 61. "I can see him now, a bronzed lithe, grey-haired old man, looking as fit as a thirty-year-old and stripped down to a pair of shorts. He pranced and skipped, waving his arms and prattling on about flying. A few of the boys giggled. Somebody elbowed me in the ribs and said 'Get on to this bloke, Herb. He's a nut' " (p. 26).*

After Elliott won the mile later that day in a time of 4:22, Cerutty asked for an introduction and said "That was a wonderful run of yours . . . there's not a shadow of doubt . . . within two years you will run a mile in four minutes" (p. 26). Like his pals, Elliott figured maybe the old coach was a little unbalanced.

Shortly after their first meeting, Elliott crushed two metatarsal bones in his right foot when helping to move a piano on stage just before his end-of-term school ball. Not only didn't he dance, he was immobilized for four months; instead of competing, he turned

---

*An almost identical reaction was experienced by Lon Spurrier in 1956 in the Olympic Village at the Melbourne Games. The U.S.A. distance runners had asked Cerutty to talk to them, and Spurrier, world record holder in the half mile, was driven by curiosity to attend the informal meeting. "To demonstrate his methods, Percy stripped down to his briefs and charged around like a man possessed," according to Spurrier. "I felt embarrassed for him and left early" (personal communication, November 9, 1990).

18 watching the 1956 Australian championships and Olympic trials outside the oval. The idleness took its toll both mentally and physically. Elliott began smoking, lost interest in running, and looked for fun where he could get it. His apathy ran rampant, and more than a year lapsed between his races. He had no goals.

The Olympic Games in Melbourne, however, provided essential and timely inspiration for Elliott. Credit must go to his parents for taking him to the Games. He recalls two telling memories from the experience:

> Of all my memories of the '56 Games the one that burns deepest is of the unathletic looking Russian sailor, Vladimir Kuts, his arms flailing and blond hair flapping, running his opposition into the red cinders during the 5000 metres and 10,000 metres. The ruthless determination in his hatchet face held everyone spellbound. We could see that he was tired and yet he tortured himself by continual bursts of sprinting. (Elliott, 1960, p. 30)

The second moment came after Kuts's 10,000-meter race. A friend of Herb's dad turned to the youngster and said, " 'If I had your ability and I'd seen this bloke running that would be the last cigarette I'd ever smoke.' "

Knowing his son was inspired by the Games, and especially by the exhausting Kuts, Herb's dad arranged a visit to Cerutty's little home a couple of miles outside Melbourne. Cerutty didn't urge Elliott to join him and his band of runners; rather, he simply talked at length about his philosophy and the life his runners led training at Portsea. Cerutty's words worked their charm, however. When Herb's mother reluctantly said he could remain in Melbourne to train with Cerutty, the running world changed, and the scrub half-acre at Portsea became one of the most talked about training spots in the world.

Upon joining the American athletes Dean Thackeray, John Kelly, and Al Hall, and the New Zealander Murray Halberg that first weekend at Portsea, Elliott (1960) described feeling "as Cortez must have felt when he viewed the Pacific Ocean" (p. 32). When he visited the little ski hut where running greats like John Landy, Les Perry, Dave Stephens, and Don MacMillan had slept, Elliott said he could "smell their sweat" and "from that day [his] dedication to running was assured" (p. 32).

Days later, Elliott snuck into the Olympic Village and was introduced to Ron Delany who had out-kicked John Landy for the gold medal in the mile. Chipper Delany slapped Elliott on the back and said "Well me bhoyo, and it looks as if oi'll be seein' you in Rome ('60 Olympics), from what oi've heard." According to Elliott (1960),

> A newspaperman, who'd learned of the Spartan training pro-gramme I'd planned, told Delany about it and he seemed shocked. Then he was told that I'd already run a mile in 4:20.4. The Irishman shook his head sadly and said, "Really now? Oi think it's wrong to start so soon. To be sure, oi couldn't run a quarter in fifty-five seconds when oi was Herb's age." (p. 33)

But Delany was in for a surprise, for Elliott was on the verge of an athletic rise previously unknown to the running world. Not four, but two years later, not 1960 in Rome but 1958 in Compton, California, and again in Dublin, Ireland, Ron Delany "would shake his head sadly" again because of young Herb.

Getting on Track

The flurry of training and racing in the last few months of Elliott's eighteenth year gave no indication of his 14-month layoff. For the record, he had won his last mile race (October 29, 1955) at the age of 17 in 4:20.4 at the state Schoolboy Championships, to remain undefeated in the mile. On January 12, 1957, he entered his first mile competition merely three months into his new training regime, and set a new world junior record (under 19 years of age) in 4:06. Elliott's time cut eight-tenths of a second off Ron Clarke's previous record. The 14-second plunge in his own time, however, was equally astounding, and John Landy who witnessed the run said, " 'Elliott is the most fantastic junior I have ever seen. He looks as though he's been running in top company for years' " (Elliott, 1960, p. 50). Within six weeks, Elliott broke the world junior records in the half mile (by 1.5 seconds under Don Bowden's record time), the two mile, and the three mile, and he also reduced his own world junior mile record time to 4:04.4. There was no doubt he was ready for the world's top runners, and unfortunately for them, they were conveniently at hand.

On March 9, 1957, and only two weeks past his 19th birthday, young Elliott was pitted against Merv Lincoln in the Australian Amateur Athletic Championships. Lincoln was widely heralded as the new king of the milers, as gentleman John Landy had stopped running, and Ron Delany was less active and back in school in the U.S. Elliott ran the race just as he had practiced it in his mind and on his feet many times. After completing three laps on his "home made" grass ovals, Elliott would yell out "Ding a-ling-a-ling" and instinctively fly into a sprint for the last lap. Elliott's sprint on March 9 carried the day against Lincoln's, and Elliott won in 4:00.4. The world was shocked at the upset, and no one was more bitterly disappointed than Franz Stampfl, Lincoln's famous coach and Cerutty's archenemy.

Austrian-born Stampfl had coached in England before being invited to Australia as its only paid University Athletic Adviser. He had met and influenced (but not actually coached) Roger Bannister. His greats included such runners as Chris Chataway, and Brian Hewson, as well as Lincoln and others. Cerutty greatly resented Stampfl and the rejection Stampfl's appointment in his homeland implied. Their mutual disrespect and disdain fueled the sports stories about their protégés' races. Elliott's race against Lincoln was the first direct confrontation pitting Stampfl's "scientific, stop-watch interval methods" against Cerutty's unorthodox "instinctive back to nature methods." The personal feud between Stampfl and Cerutty would run hot and fierce, fired through news commentary and sports gossip as Lincoln and Elliott repeated a series of eight head-to-head mile races. Elliott and Cerutty triumphed together each time.

Camp Life

The meteoric athletic rise of young Elliott leaves no doubt that the arranged visit at Cerutty's home was a key turning point in his life. Cerutty's first prediction to Herb at Aquinas in 1955 had left the young man and his pals thinking that maybe the old coach was nuts. But it had come true. Herb had run a four-minute mile within two years. Now Cerutty was telling Herb he would find joy through strength, just as the coach had experienced himself. And again Herb was finding that true, as he was Cerutty's words that sacrifice and pain were the essence of training.

Portsea was the back-to-nature haven where pain and sacrifice were endured in new ways, and the soft ways of urban living forgotten. Everything about the camp was raw and rugged—the terrain, the huts and bunks, the food, the runners, and above all the coach. There was a free spirit atmosphere to the place, but it was quite unlike the lifestyles of later generations of free spirits.

Pain, not euphoria, set the tone of Cerutty's camp, and he preached on and on about it. " 'Pain is the purifier . . . thrust against pain.' " He had the men read about Saint Francis of Assisi, and, in the spirit of those readings, Cerutty continued, " 'Walk towards suffering, Love suffering, Embrace it' " (Elliott, 1960, p. 38).

Camp rules prohibited nicotine, alcohol, and women companions. Pubs and cinemas were off limits, and no one was allowed away from the camp's center for any purpose other than training without Cerutty's permission. Bill Lacy, one of the athletes in camp with Elliott, wrote a poem about Cerutty's regime:

> A runner stood at the Pearly Gates,
> His face was worn and old,
> He bravely asked the man of fate
> Admission to the fold.

> "What have you done," St. Peter said?
> "To seek an entrance here."
> "I trained at Portsea, that was my task,
> For many and many a year!"

> Then wide the gates did open,
> The angels clanged their bell.
> "Come in and take a harp," he said,
> "You've had enough of Hell."
> (cited in Elliott, 1960, p. 44)

The daily schedule, though informal, took on a fairly regular pattern, and according to Elliott (1960), a typical day went like this.

7 a.m.—A five-mile run before breakfast in any direction our whim took us, followed by a dip in the ocean.

8 a.m.—Breakfast of uncooked rolled oats (without milk) sprinkled with wheat germ, walnuts, sultanas, raisins and sliced banana. Perhaps a few potato chips to follow.

9 a.m.—Swimming and surfing or outdoor chores like chopping wood, painting and carpentry.

Noon—Training and lectures at Portsea Oval, followed by another swim.

2 p.m.—Lunch—fish and fresh fruit.

3 p.m.—Siesta

4 p.m.—Weight lifting.

5 p.m.—Ten-mile run along dirt roads ending once more at the beach.

7 p.m.—Tea and a general discussion led by Percy on a wide variety of subjects.

11 p.m.—Lights out. (p. 45)

Don Connery put a more literary touch to the description of a typical day for Elliott at Portsea. Connery's 1958 *Sports Illustrated* article was subtitled "Led by a fanatic and driven by private furies, Australia's fantastic miler finds solace and satisfaction in pushing himself beyond endurance." Then Connery opened with his description of the Portsea ordeal:

On a primeval, wind-swept beach at Portsea, a curling tongue of scruffy Cape Cod land 60 miles south of Melbourne, a slender Australian clerk with a Dick Tracy nose and a tanned body of sinewy steel sprints a final hundred yards and slumps to the golden sand. Dragging in his foot-steps like the exhausted survivors of a desert march come a boilermaker, shoemaker, architect, draftsman and a panting Dalmatian.

Catching his breath after the chill morning's 14-mile gallop down a sandy road, round and round the rolling Portsea golf course and along the broad beach, the leggy clerk revives suddenly. He kicks off his trunks and moldy track shoes, and plunges into the frigid waters of the Bass Strait. The others follow dazedly and thrash with him in the foaming breakers. Then he leads them, clothing in hand, in a naked single file through a forest of looming, unruly sand dunes. At the largest dune, he grunts at the 60° slope, then alone churns up the grueling 80 feet. (On another day, more refreshed, he had mounted the dune a record 42 times in succession.) Muscles now worked to the limit, he leads the troupe of young athletes through scrub and roots and over barbed-wire fences to a clapboard "ski hut" surrounded by rusty barrels, empty paint cans and orange peels. They dart into a cold shower, then collapse into bunks and sleeping bags. But within half an hour, as if someone had turned on the juice, the clerk is up again.

Refueling on raw carrots, cabbage, brown bread, cheese and milk, he cuts around the stunted tea trees to a grove marked "muscle tougheners" and begins hefting barbells and heavy slabs of rail.

Thus does Herbert James Elliott, 20, world's fastest man, owner of the international mile and 1,500-meter track records and already preserved in wax at Madame Tussaud's, work off the problems and frustrations of success with deliberate tortures of the body. A man who seems to find in prolonged and superhuman effort the isolation from the public and private furies which possess him, Elliott is the prototype of the modern super-athlete who seems destined to go far beyond the limits of what hitherto has been considered tolerable for the human physique. (pp. 67-68)

As these descriptions suggest, Cerutty demanded total dedication of each runner. Each was directed to set a specific individual goal. Cerutty told Elliott that joining him would mean " 'buckling down to a life of sacrifice,' " and he added, " 'I'm not interested in athletics, I'm only interested in achievement. Fix your goal and work for it,' " he said (Elliott, 1960, p. 43). Elliott did. He wanted to be the world's best miler.

Part of the total dedication unique to Cerutty's methods was the diet of mostly raw foods. "Cooking kills" was the title of a pamphlet on diet that Percy wrote in the 1950s, and his carbohydrate emphasis was decades ahead of the times, nutritionally speaking. The breakfast of Cerutty's champions was not milk and Wheaties. Rolled oats, nuts, dried fruits, bananas, raw cabbage, brown bread, and cheese were Portsea staples.

Weight lifting was another special feature of Cerutty's methods. He and Harry Hopman, who introduced weight training to tennis, revolutionized training in their respective sports. According to Elliott, they were largely responsible for the eminence Australia enjoyed in both tennis and running at that time. They exploded the fallacy that weight lifting made athletes muscle-bound. Cerutty made the strong-legged, skinny-bodied runner a thing of the past. His runners had powerful arms and shoulders. Indeed, in running every part of the body is subject to strain, and weights help build the strength and power to overcome the strain. Heavy rather than light weights were used as a means to the end, the goals of running and winning.

Three landmarks were of special importance at Portsea, beginning with the 80-foot sand hill. Elliott's best effort of 42 times up and down in succession stood well, but Ian Beck had doubled that number. The record time up the dune was 11 seconds, held by Russell Mockridge, an Olympic cyclist and friend of Elliott's, who was killed in the late 1950s in a collision with a bus.

The second landmark was the Hall Circuit. It was one mile and 285 yards of sandy trails that wound up and down. Every one in camp was tested on it, and Elliott (1960) claims that "The atmosphere on the eve of an attack on Hall Circuit was more tense than for an Australian championship" (p. 43). Landy would never break six minutes, and Cerutty's best time was 7:44. The best times in Elliott's era (as of 1960) were

5:21.4—Herb Elliott

5:30.0—Ian Beck

5:31.0—Don Brain

5:39.0—Dean Thackeray

5:40.7—Robbie Morgan-Morris

5:43.0—Denis Wilson

5:43.8—Doug Chugg

5:48.0—Laurie Elliott

5:50.0—Geoff Fleming

5:51.0—Alex Henderson

5:52.0—Brian Curle

The third landmark was the Stewart Circuit, a quarter-mile, undulating course that finished at the top of a steep hill. A Trinidad sprinter named Mike Agostini was the only one to break 60 seconds over Stewart Circuit.

Roadways, parks, golf courses, and other natural terrain were used as well, but tracks were seldom used except for races. In addition, there was the ever present pounding surf, and Cerutty routinely had the runners pour into the water, regardless of the season or weather. The purpose was to build mental toughness and determination. It also almost killed Cerutty. In a practice run one day over the Hall Circuit, Cerutty took a few shortcuts to make the run competitive, and beat Elliott to the beach. Cerutty yelled, " 'Well, I beat you today and I'll beat you in a swim too!' " Then

Cerutty flung himself into the surf only to get caught in a strong riptide. As he was helplessly swept out, his energy finally expired. Elliott (1960) described the scene:

> He was about 150 yards from the shore and every time a wave went over him he'd stay down until I was sure he was drowned. Then his white mane appeared for a second until the next wave engulfed him. When finally I reached him I employed the method of pushing him along and keeping his head up. Then my feet struck a sandbank.
>
> "You beauty!" I gasped. Picking Percy up in my arms, I carried him along the sandbank, horizontal to the shore, and then back through the rocks to the shore. As we reached the beach, Percy said tersely, "Put me down at once." Realizing that my old mentor's pride was hurt, I did as he commanded. He looked green, he was so spent, but he wouldn't let anyone touch him. He lay on that beach for one hour, during which I ran to the camp to fetch Nancy, his wife, who then sat by his side, comforting him.
>
> "I'll try to get back to the camp now," he said as the colour returned to his face. He brushed aside our hands and walked slowly to the top of the sandhills. There he sagged to his knees and fell asleep for half an hour while we watched over him. At last he got up and—indomitable to the end—stumbled back unaided to the camp. Percy knew, and we all knew, that he had been very close to death. (pp. 65-66)

Though his pride was tarnished, the incident did not change Cerutty's back-to-nature philosophy or his application of it. He continued to execute his belief " 'that no matter how cold it is you must expose your body to the air at least once a day and surf right through winter' " (Elliott, 1960, p. 39).

No one in camp could surpass Cerutty's will to win, competitiveness, and determination. And he could handle almost any challenge "on call." Lafayette Smith (1960) tells of a special moment in early 1960.

> Not long ago Percy was timing Elliott and several other runners on a grass track at Portsea when another athlete appeared with a newspaper clipping from America. It described how Joie Ray of East Gary, Indiana, a world champion miler before World

War I, always ran a mile on his birthday. That year, at age 64, he had run it in 5:50 and the papers had heralded the achievement as a "world's record for men over 60."

Percy calmly handed his stop watch to Elliott and trotted quickly four times around the quarter-mile track. Panting heavily he asked Elliott: "What does the watch say?"

"5:32.5," said the young miler.

"So much for Ray's record," triumphed Cerutty. "Now, back to the workout." (p. 133)*

Stotan Creed by Word and Deed

Highly emotional Cerutty could inspire athletes like few other coaches. He was both a talker and a doer, and his words and exploits released powers in the minds and souls of others. He firmly believed that if anybody intended to show a group how to do something, he must be prepared to do it first himself. Before important races, Cerutty would simulate the anticipated experience with a race of his own. Elliott (1960) reports the effects of his coaches' demonstrations.

> [He'd run] usually the equivalent of a mile, with all the speed he could muster, and then stagger over to me, eyes bulging and tongue lolling. "Well, you may be able to run faster," he'd gasp, "but tomorrow you can't run any harder than that." Remembering he was in his sixties, I often felt alarmed by his exertions. . . .
>
> To me, Percy's own life, his own struggle for achievement in the face of depressing handicaps, posed a challenge. With limited physical resources, he's courageously whipped himself to perform almost frightening athletic feats. I reckoned that if I didn't try to punish my young, strong body as he did his older body I'd despise myself. (p. 36)

Cerutty helped his runners to world records not so much through improvements in their techniques as through their spirit. As he boasted, " 'I raise the spirits of the athlete and inspire the soul to

*Joe Ray and Percy were within a few months of each other in age.

a higher state of consciousness. As the athlete grows spiritually as a person, his performance in the physical will gradually unfold to new heights' " (Elliott, 1960, p. 168).

He labeled the core of his philosophy and creed *Stotan*, a word he coined from the words Stoic and Spartan. His nightly campfire discussions, and his many lectures and demonstrations beat on the themes of nature, self-reliance, strength, and determination. Cerutty explained the Stotan creed this way:

> "Stotans," ordained Percy, "will, by virtue of their philosophy, be nature lovers, with a respect and appreciation of all evolved or created things. They will appreciate the sanctity of creative effort both in themselves and in others. They will strive to understand the significance implied by reality, will be able to discern the real from the spurious, and see no anomaly in nudity, either in body or mind. But neither will they cast pearls before swine. Stotans, for all the reasons that their philosophy stands for—hardness, toughness, unswerving devotion to an ideal, and many more—will look upon the sea as their pristine element and endeavor to associate themselves with their prime-val source of life by going into the sea at least once per month in all seasons of the year. No practice is more disposed to toughen both the body and the morale than this. Stotans believe that neither the body nor mind can be maintained at a high pitch of efficiency unless sufficient regular rest is obtained, and aim at a daily average of eight hours sleep (that is for young men—older men need only six hours). Stotans also will not be found in social places after midnight. Stotans shall regulate their lives so that at the end of a period, varying with the intensity of the effort, each shall realize that he has attained, without conscious striving, a state of knowledge and a position of leadership in the community. It is axiomatic that only the pure can understand purity, only the cultivated appreciate beauty, and only the strong measure their strength. Therefore, only the self-disciplined can command genuine respect. (Elliott, 1960, p. 38)

What a creed it was—strange, simplistic common sense, and yet unique! Central to Cerutty's message was an appreciation of nature—" 'You've got to woo nature like a sweetheart' " (Elliott, 1960, p. 39), he said. Elaborating, he added

"My Stotan philosophy is based on communication with nature. This communication takes place when the person sleeps under the stars at night, hears the birds in the morning, feels the sand between his toes, smells the flowers, hears the surf. Nature can bring the mind and body into perfect harmony and balance with the universe. This is one of the factors that allows the athlete to reach new levels of excellence." (Myers, 1977, p. 169)

He lectured that " 'The future, or destiny is a projection of ourselves and our intrinsic worth' " (p. 169), but reminded the men that most people neglect to pursue their potential. At Portsea, Cerutty advanced and accelerated each athlete toward his individual destiny by focusing him mentally and spiritually on his destiny full time. And this total dedication was immersed in the forces of nature provided in the sand and surf of Portsea.

Cerutty abhorred regimented styles of training and refused to write training schedules for the runners. Instead, he tried to build an attitude of finding your own way, knowing yourself, and building from there. Each runner set his own goals and training schedules.

"The mastery of the true self," Percy said, "and the refusal to permit others to dominate us is the ultimate in living, and self-expression in athletics. The truly great in any field of endeavor never needed flatteries, adulations or the rewards that are bestowed upon them. To feel a contempt for the bestower is a concomitant and greatness!" (Myers, 1977, p. 169)

The total dedication approach demanded by Cerutty disciplined the runners to compete instinctively. The idea was to soar above the common herd of runners by virtue of superior willpower, strength, and confidence. The confidence the runners gained at Portsea necessitated no strategies for races. Cerutty's runners feared no man.

Elliott (1960) explained the importance of year round training with Cerutty this way: "The main thing about Percy is that he coaches your spirit." Elliott believed "The body itself may only need two months training to get fit; the rest of the time you're building up your spirit—call it guts, or some inner force—so that it will go to work for you in a race without your even knowing it" (p. 39). Elliott believed that athletes who resort to tactics in a race, or a plan of tactics, had no real confidence. His only tactic was to approach a race determined to win.

Shaking hands after a race was considered appropriate and sporting, but Elliott and Cerutty thought it hypocritical to shake opponents' hands and wish them luck before the race. Cerutty believed that you must make yourself ferocious to gain maximum effort. He said, " 'While a man is racing he must hate himself and his competitors' " (Elliott, 1960, p. 146). No harm was intended, just faster running.

Mixed into his lectures and demonstrations were his poetry and essays—for inspiration. After his noontime talks to the men, Cerutty often encouraged them to go in separate directions and be alone to practice what they had heard. He told each of them "to clean the venom out of his system" (Myers, 1977, p. 170).

Cerutty understood first hand that the process of achieving success is long and arduous. It is mostly work and focused dedication. He said,

> "You can't win if you don't start doing something about your goal right now. Success and achievement awaits he who can grasp it. If the athlete wants to become an Olympic champion, he must work hard at his event, even if it means working for years to reach the goal. Work does things. Hard things take time to do. Impossible things take a little longer. *Patience* and *persistence* are the key words to success in athletics. There is never any hurry on the creative plane!" (Myers, 1977, p. 172)

> "No one is born great," Percy said. "He may be born to become great. Destiny and fate have a miraculous way of working things out to bring tremendous results." (p. 170)

> "To be great in any event in track and field," Percy said, "the person's life must be a masterpiece like a great work of art."

> It bothered Percy that most people seemed so afraid to let their personalities stand naked, that so many people clung to secret hopes and dreams that would never surface, and which would only cause anxiety and frustration. People are much more energetic and ambitious, he believed, when they find an outlet for their emotions. For the athletes at Portsea, that outlet was running, jumping and throwing. For most people, the outlet is never found.

> Lack of immediate success is the most common reason why people give up their goals. But failure should always be looked upon positively, not negatively.

"If an athlete wants to be an Olympic champion, he must cleave to his destiny, and work hard until he achieves his goal. When the person works hard each day, he will find the way that will bring him one step closer to satisfying his goals. Thought is born from failure! Only when the person's actions fail to satisfy his basic needs is there grounds for serious thought. The greater the failure, the more soul-searching that is needed for success in the future," Percy said.

Success should never be gauged just in terms of records or victories. Success should be measured by how much the person enjoys what he is doing and to what degree he is striving to do his best. (p. 171)

It merits emphasis to recognize how close are Cerutty's thoughts on winning, success, and striving to Wooden's (peace of mind) and Lombardi's ("winning isn't everything but making the effort to win is").

The Cerutty Virus

By the Olympic Year 1960, milers and distance runners all over the world were catching the Cerutty virus. Running barefooted became a fad, training in sand caught on, diets changed, and upperbody work was taken seriously.* With all eyes on Elliott, serious runners, and especially Olympic hopefuls, were striving for the toughness Cerutty's ways realized.

An example of the Cerutty virus was provided in picture and verse in a March 28, 1960 *Sports Illustrated* article entitled, "Ron and Don by the Sea." The American great, Don Bowden, who had visited Cerutty briefly in 1959, learned firsthand that he was not competitive over Hall Circuit, and Cerutty admonished him to use weights and take up resistance running. Ron Delany, who was also training in California for the Olympics, often ran with Bowden on weekends. The article showed them together by the sea, running

---

*George Linn, a star high school and collegiate miler and my roommate at Cal, went to Portsea for six months our freshman year (1959-1960) to train with Cerutty and the men in camp. Through George, Cerutty even influenced me, and my mother was astonished when she first learned I was regularly eating raw oats.

barefooted, challenging nature, tearing up the sand dunes and down the beaches. The author, Robert Boyle (1960) wrote

> With Elliott on their minds. . . . They reached the peak of the dune—it must be at least 300 feet high—and sprinted down the precipitous forward slope to the beach. They ran along the water's edge together until they disappeared into a blanket of fog. A half hour later they appeared again. Bowden sat down at the base of the dune and took off his shoes and socks, as Delany did push-ups before sprinting down the beach alone. Bowden got up and ran into the water. He ran up and down in the surf, lifting his knees high. Delany returned and took his shoes off. Bowden joined him, and they sprinted back and forth on the wet sand. Then they assaulted the dune, their feet slipping in the loose sand. They reached the top and ran down the other side. Then they ran back up again.

> "What does this sand-dune running do for you?" Delany was asked.

> "It makes you feel sick," he exclaimed.

> "It destroys morale and builds up physical capabilities," said Bowden. "I think I'm king of the mountain when I reach the top here. I'd love to take Elliott here when he comes over. Don't you think he'd enjoy it, Ron?"

> Ron, with a weary smile, "Oh, he'd love it."

> They ran down to the beach again. "Ah," said Delany, "this gets you away from civilization for a weekend. No one to bother you. No one with model airplanes trying to gun you down."

> "It's restful and relaxing and a change of scenery," said Bowden. (p. 27)

Another Olympic hopeful and America's top miler in 1960 was Dyrol Burleson of the University of Oregon. *Sports Illustrated* (May 30, 1960) acknowledged Cerutty's influence on Burleson and indeed the entire Oregon running program this way: "Last week Dyrol Burleson trained hard and long despite torrential rains that drenched Oregon, and he won the mile in a conference meet on Saturday. Burleson's coach, Bill Bowerman, sounding like Cerutty, said, 'The rains didn't bother Burleson. There's no such thing as bad weather, just soft people' " (Maule, 1960, p. 10).

That *Sports Illustrated* article, entitled "The New Herb Elliott" raised doubts, however, about Elliott. Pictured eating soft foods and drinking soft drinks during his 1960 solo tour of California, where three races had been scheduled, Elliott didn't appear the awesome figure he portrayed in 1958. Cerutty's absence raised questions about their relationship, and Elliott was now married and had a newborn son. His pulling out of one race because of an injury and running mediocre but winning times in the other two had the world wondering. Without Cerutty was Herb Elliott beatable? Every top miler was gunning for him and for the chance to break his unbeaten streak of mile wins. The world looked to Rome as Elliott returned to Melbourne in June for final preparations for the Games.

The detected rift between Cerutty and Elliott was in fact real and had been festering for almost a year. Elliott's interests had widened, and he frequented Portsea less and less often. "Cerutty blasts Herb Elliott" read a newspaper poster near the end of the 1959 Australian winter. Cerutty charged Elliott with becoming lazy, and suggested he might even have a tough time gaining selection to the Australian Olympic team. Their rift did not lead to rupture, however. Elliott (1960) admitted Cerutty was right "when he hinted that the old dedication to running had vanished" (p. 124), but Elliott still had the Cerutty virus and an uncanny faith in himself and in Cerutty. As he had told reporters who were questioning his condition in May, " 'I have a backlog of strength from the years with Cerutty,' he said. 'You develop physical and mental strength when you train that way, you know. Even when I'm not completely fit, I can call on that. Once in a while, for one reason or another, it won't be there, but most often it is' " (Maule, 1960, p. 13).

Elliott also recognized that if he wanted the gold medal in Rome, he had stretched his time without Cerutty to the limits. Like a softening America, he worried that "When you have made it, when you are sitting on top of the world . . . you need the prodding . . . to ensure you don't fall off your perch. Certainly, I felt before the 1960 Games that I needed Percy's inspiration more than I could remember needing it when I was a young and dedicated athlete" (Elliott, 1960, p. 43).

Early in June, he embarked on the final stages of his preparation for Rome and to eliminate his sporadic moments of self-doubt. Returning to Portsea and Cerutty was the winning way. As Elliott (1960) explained it,

More than ever Percy was needed to emphasize and re-emphasize that running was an expression of the body, not a tedious chore; that endless running should be indulged in for the benefits derived from the sweat and pain of vigorous exercise. A few week-end visits to Portsea were well worthwhile, as these excerpts from my diary show:

"13th June: At midday Percy gave his lecture down at the Oval. He is like an oasis in the desert of my lost enthusiasm. After listening to him talk I ran four miles round the track with the galloping action that he advocates." (After a long study of

c   b   a

f   e   d

Percy demonstrating his new form of exaggerated galloping running. The runner inhales during the first phase (a-c) and exhales during the second phase (d-f). Herb Elliot practiced this form at Portsea shortly before his 1960 Olympic triumph.

animals in motion Percy believes that a rhythmic galloping action will revolutionize middle distance running.)

"14th June: Listening to Percy talk at the week-end did me a lot of good—always run hard so that you can be satisfied at the completion of the run. Remember you are training to achieve a goal. Be certain that each run leads you closer to the goal." (pp. 159-160)

On August 1, Elliott's confidence skyrocketed when he broke his previous best time over Hall Circuit by seven seconds. Although he had not experienced top-class competition in the months leading up to the Games, he knew now that he was ready.

After arriving in Rome, Elliott confirmed his self-confidence by easily winning his heats. An injured Bowden (Achilles tendon) was not there, and Delany had opted to run the half-mile, but the final eight pitted the world's best against the only man ever to remain undefeated in the mile. Shortly after Elliott's first visit to Portsea, he had marked September 6, 1960 in his calendar as *his day*. Now September 6 had arrived. During the 3 minutes and 35.6 seconds it took Elliott to win the 1500-meter gold medal, the odd couple from down under were both true to form. No one had thought it possible after the grueling trials that anyone could set a new world record, but Elliott had not only done the unbelievable, he beat six others who also broke the equivalent of the four-minute mile. The first six runners, including Dyrol Burleson (U.S.), had beat Delany's 1956 Olympic record. Moreover, Elliott had beat the second place runner, Jazy of France, by nearly 20 yards, the largest winning margin in the modern history of the Games. But Cerutty, who had forecast and orchestrated Elliott's victory and record, wasn't surprised. As Elliott (1960) described it,

When I learned that a new world mark of 3:35.6 had been set I remembered with gratitude Percy. It was scarcely credible, as the officials were insisting, that he'd been waving his towel [his world record signal] to me from the side of the track. He'd gone to great pains before the race to point out to me precisely where in the crowd he would be standing and so deeply must I have been concentrating that when the image of him swirling his towel flashed before me it didn't occur that he *wasn't* standing in the crowd. It appeared, however, that Percy hadn't wanted to take any chance of not being seen and had hopped over a moat (a formidable barrier intended to discourage the most excitable Italian spectator from joining the athletes on the arena) to do his signalling by the trackside. Unbeknown to me at the time, a couple of policemen carted him off rather forcibly—but not before he'd completed the job he'd set his heart on doing. (pp. 176-177)

Roger Bannister, the first human to break the four-minute barrier, personally timed Elliott on the same watch that recorded his own historic achievement. As Bannister (1960) authoritatively wrote for *Sports Illustrated*, "No other athlete in Rome commanded such superiority over his rivals, no other athlete emerged with that elusive magic of victory which the Greeks sought, in such abundance" (p. 28). As recognized by Bannister and other giants of the sport, Elliott had come as close to running perfection as the world has ever known. He accomplished this at the age of 22, years before the prime of a miler.

To see this in perspective, we must recall that after 1880 when W.G. George set the world record in a time of 4:12, 50 years elapsed before the 4:10 limit was broken. Fifty years to gain two seconds! By 1943, Gundar Haag had lowered the record to 4:01.4. Eleven years later, Bannister lowered it another two seconds, and John Landy reduced it another second in 1956. Then Elliott took up with Cerutty. In less than four years, they in effect knocked six seconds off the record. Elliott raced the mile (and/or 1500 meters) 32 times between 1957 and 1960. He was never defeated. Indeed, even throughout his younger years he was never defeated at that distance. After Rome, he and his wife Ann and baby son moved to England where he attended college at Cambridge. Later they returned home, but to new horizons. Herb Elliott never raced again.

In contrast, Cerutty persisted with his rugged-life philosophy right up to his death in 1975. By then, Queen Elizabeth had honored him with the Member of the British Empire Award, and Cerutty's scrub half-acre at Portsea had become known officially as the International Health, Athletic, and Fitness Center. Shortly before he died at age 80, he was stronger than when he had embarked on his new life at age 43.

In the 23 years Cerutty actively coached at Portsea, 30 world record breakers followed his methods and fell victim to the Cerutty virus. Some men thought him a crank, many viewed him skeptically, but all agreed he was unique. A philosopher and poet, an athlete and coach, and above all an individual, Percy Cerutty was a force in athletics like few others. Cerutty and his Stotans raised horizons and pushed forward our conceptions of human limits. They did it by living and believing in the Stotan Creed.

Chapter 7

The Essence
of Philosopher Coaching

A Dying Breed?

The lineage of philosopher coaches is in peril, threatened by the march of time and the changing environment of sports. The growing organizational complexity and commercialization of athletics in pro teams and institutions of higher learning have changed the mix of skills required and sought in coaches. So have the sizes of the paychecks.

The special virtues and characteristics of the philosopher coach are being smothered by the new, additional talents needed to win and promote the game. No one is to blame. It is not the fault of the coaches, nor the players, team owners, or fans. The changing character of coaching is being driven by the market place, by the growing number of fans willing and able to pay top dollar for sports entertainment, by technical progress in the development of athletes, and by the media. These forces are pulling the modern head coach in directions different in both scope and intensity than coaches of earlier generations.

When a university president and athletic director pick their head football or basketball coach the stakes are high—higher today than ever before. Consider the implications of the coaching selection at Ohio State or Indiana or any major NCAA university. Students and

157

alumni take pride in their teams and the national media forcefully remind them of their national and league standing on a week-by-week basis. The media don't report the coach's standing as an educator or expand on his contributions to the human development of student athletes. The media report the team's wins and losses, the glories and disappointments of the games, and the coach is publicly held accountable each week. Rules infractions claim headlines, and violations generate stormy periods for the guilty and innocent alike.

The money at stake in big time intercollegiate athletics is not just from ticket sales or revenues from nationally televised games, lucrative though they are. Big money also comes from alumni donations, from old timers who are contemplating their wills, or from graduates who are active in sports booster clubs and other university affairs. Add to these financial considerations the impact of alumni and sports enthusiasts who are state legislators pondering budgetary decisions for higher education in their states, and the stakes are raised again. In Columbus, Ohio, and Indianapolis, Indiana and their hinterlands, the passion for victory is high, and the money flows to the victorious.

Experts on management often chastise U.S. corporations for being shortsighted. They note critically that top managers aim too much at short-run profits at the expense of long-term planning and preparation. Alternatively stated, long-term planning flies in the face of many financial incentive and reward schemes. This short-run bias results when promotions and pay incentives are geared to quarterly reports—about the time span of a whole season for a typical coach.

The soundness of this criticism is widely acknowledged. But, compared to a coach's predicament, the corporate world's allotment of time is long indeed. How much time can a coach afford to spend for long-term planning needed to conceptualize a novel brand of play or a new approach to the game—a pyramid of success, a hierarchy of needs, or a Stotan creed?

A beginning coach can often survive one bad season and sometimes two, but three is a dead sure way of getting fired. In performance time, big-ticket coaches have about three-quarters of a corporate year to prove themselves. Even a patient university president and athletic director can't hold back the pressure to make a change if losses persist. Their jobs are on the line, too. A new coach knows he has to win games, right now.

In the first rush of responsibilities, a new head coach must gather together a competent staff of assistant coaches. In big time football, this requires the talent to select and effectively organize and manage a large staff. However, after coaching assignments are made and tasks are delegated, a wedge is driven between the head coach's responsibilities and the assistants' actions. An important element of control and sense of responsibility is lost.

The next major task of a coach is to recruit new athletes. If an assistant coach skirts the rules to attract a top athlete—without getting caught, of course—shouldn't the head coach look the other way? What if a few helpful alumni provide some favors—on their own, naturally? How can the coach control them? Top talent is vital, and aren't other teams cheating on the rules? Isn't it OK to do so too—for the university, of course—as long as no one finds out? And aren't many of the rules silly anyway?

To be a head coach of a clean program requires not only strong ethical values and an iron will, but strong managerial skills, as well. Subordinates must be closely watched as well as cleverly, if not virtuously, led. The time needed and the stress inflicted take their toll on the person in charge.

The technical knowledge required to coach has also grown, and, to be competitive, coaches must employ far more sophisticated training methods than were required years ago. Attendance at coaching clinics is essential to stay abreast of these new methods and technical advances. Who has time for philosophizing about sports, life, and the quest for human progress when there's barely time for teaching essential modern methods on how to win? Who has time for mediocre or troublesome athletes—for Gary Waltons, or Proverb Jacobs? Who has time for "paying forward" or putting things in "proper perspective"?

The travel schedule for team competition and recruiting has been augmented by the growing number of public speaking engagements of coaches. In addition, a coach is now sidetracked by the art of media relations. A regular TV show hosted by the coach pays big bucks and solidifies the alumni who are regular viewers. Public speaking at fundraisers for the university brings in lots of money, too. Tell us coach, please, are we going to a bowl game this year? Where is the time for poems and legends, for letters and phone calls to graduates, for stories to hospitalized children? Hadn't a coach better spend his time fundraising, or recruiting, or planning for the next game or the next season?

As these polemics suggest, the job description of a head football or basketball coach at a major university in the 1990s is different than it was at mid-century. People attracted to these important positions today bring a different array of skills. The importance of leadership and education still exists, but other roles compete for the scarce time available, and there is less time for a coach to provide personal direction to student athletes. And the stress is causing an alarming number of coaches to depart the profession early.

On October 9, 1989, *Newsweek* ran a story by Tom Callahan entitled: "The Fall of the Genius Coach: Ten Years Are All a Body Can Stand." Beginning with the opening paragraph, here are some excerpts:

> Where have all the geniuses gone? Dallas has discarded Tom Landry. Chuck Noll is dangling from a Pittsburgh ledge. Miamians no longer cross themselves when they mention Don Shula. Bill Walsh has fled San Francisco and taken sanctuary with NBC. Mike Ditka is soldiering on after a heart attack in Chicago. Barry Switzer was swept away with the Oklahoma flotsam. Penn State has reclassified Joe Paterno fallible. Pro or college, the legendary football coach is in a hell of a way.

> Paterno sighs and lies to himself, "I'm not 62, I'm 52. If I were 62, I couldn't do this job." . . . In the era of crack and steroids, Paterno considers "the coach-player relationship" the hardest element to hold. "You constantly have to think back to what it was like when you were 18 and 20—before you got to be an old fogy—and try to remember some of the things you felt as a kid."

> John Madden says, "It's bigger than football. From the president on down, the guys in charge of everything used to be revered but now are lucky if they're respected. Some people are wondering why the NFL can't settle on a commissioner. I got a different question: who the heck would want to be commissioner? It has to be a brutal job, like being the coach." (p. 82)

A Modern-Day Survivor

In the summer of 1990, when John Thompson, the legendary basketball coach at Georgetown University, turned down the

6 million dollar offer to coach the Denver Nuggets, it made headline news in sports pages throughout the nation. What made it of national interest was not just the money he turned down, but his rationale. The opening line by Michael Wilbon of the *Washington Post* (June 24, 1990) captured what was newsworthy: "Perhaps the most important words spoken by John Thompson Friday were: 'I am an educator' " (p. D-4). When Robert Churchwell, a bright young recruit from Gonzaga High school in Washington, learned about the offer he said: "That's a lot of money; he's got to take it." After Thompson announced his decision to stay at Georgetown, Churchwell said, "I guess he's about a lot more than money." In taking questions from the press, Thompson elaborated on his reasoning: " 'I never felt there was nothing left to accomplish at Georgetown. I have always felt my responsibility was broader than wins and losses' " (Wilbon, 1990, p. D-4).

John Thompson is a modern-day survivor of the tantalizing offer. Although he hardly has taken vows of poverty, in many ways he has become a novelty. There are a few others like him, but how many of us have the strength of character to see a "higher order of responsibility" as a personal reward more valuable than the size of the paycheck? John Wooden was one, and on two occasions he listened long enough to receive offers to coach in the pros. He listened simply because there was so much money involved. Wooden said, " 'I felt it necessary to talk with my wife and children, to let them in on the decision,' " then laughing added, " 'although in all truthfulness I knew what they were going to say beforehand. I just didn't want to take any chances' " (Phillips, 1985, p. 44). Wooden, of course, said "no" to both offers. Both Wooden and John Thompson possess a peace of mind and sense of success in knowing that the work they do has high purpose—their profession is *guiding* the youth.

Philosopher coaches have the gifted knack of being able to step back from all the daily business to see what they're about, why they work, and what's wonderful about it. They see life as a process rather than an event. In part, this is what Cerutty meant when he said "all mankind has something special to contribute to uplifting humanity" (Meyers, 1977, p. 169). He complained that we too often neglect our potential, don't see our contributions, shortsightedly undervalue our results, and measure our contributions by our paychecks alone. Eric Hoffer added insight to this perspective: "The feeling of being hurried is not usually the result of living a full life and having no time. It is on the contrary born of a vague fear that we are wasting our life. When we do not do the one thing we ought to do, we have no time for anything else—we are the busiest people in the world." In short, Wooden and Thompson's example and Hoffer's sage advice indicate that work must mean more than a paycheck. Even a pro coach like Lombardi would have agreed. Unfortunately, it is commonplace and natural to perceive each big offer as if it were the chance of a lifetime. Dare we miss it? The lure of big time money places the coach as educator at risk and taxes the coach-player relationship.

The Common Denominator

Each great philosopher coach is unique, but there are several attributes that philosopher coaches appear to share. At the risk of oversight and possibly ridicule, I suggest ten common characteristics as listed in Table 7.1.

In the most grass roots sense, the philosopher coaches presented here were (9) straightforward, honest men of strong character. They held firmly to deeply felt moral principles and had a (1) sincere commitment to individual integrity, values, and well-rounded personal growth. Each possessed a (4) long-run perspective and commitment to their players and teams and (6) valued the coach-player relationship for more than the objective of winning. Each had a (7) special affinity for people and an understanding of human

Table 7.1
Ten Characteristics of Philosopher Coaches

1. Committed to individual integrity, values, and personal growth.
2. Profound thinkers who see themselves as educators, not just coaches.
3. Well-educated (formally and informally) in a liberal arts tradition.
4. Long-run commitment to their athletes and their institution.
5. Willing to experiment with new ideas.
6. Value the coach-player relationship, winning aside.
7. Understand and appreciate human nature.
8. Love their sport and work.
9. Honest and strong in character.
10. Human and therefore imperfect.

nature. They touched others lives positively. They (8) loved their sport and typically were workaholics with the strength of character (5) to experiment with new ideas to advance their sport. Without exception they were (2) profound thinkers, true thinking men who saw themselves more as educators than as coaches, just as John Thompson sees himself. All were (3) committed to learning and read "deeply of good books," to borrow Wooden's father's phrase. In addition to their formal education, typically in the liberal arts, they persisted in continued learning throughout their lives.

In short, philosopher coaches are like the ancient sages and philosopher kings: They are a special brand of leaders, role models for others, coaches and non-coaches alike, to follow. Faultless character and saintly morality, though ideal, are not a prerequisite for philosopher coaching, hence Category 10 in Table 7.1. Heroes and philosopher coaches are not perfect, and we threaten them all the more when we insist on white knight perfection. It should be recalled that Lombardi was a social drinker and swore like a trooper, Hamilton was a chain smoker of filterless Camels, Wooden used profanity and was viewed by some as uncompassionate, Counsilman used locker room-style vulgarity and harbored resentments, Hayes displayed a violent temper, and Cerutty was a social misfit. Yet despite their shortcomings, they provided sterling-quality leadership and examples worth following.

The Challenge

It is an irony of fate that the changes in sports that have side-tracked the philosopher coach and threatened the coach-player relationship have arisen in a time when substitutes for the philosopher coach are also diminishing. The American family now claims less authority and provides less direction for our youth than at any time in our nation's history. The decline of the church and temple has loosened the strength of religious tenants in our values, beliefs, and behavior. Our public schools have lost the confidence of many parents, and nearly a third of high school students walk away from the classroom before graduation. Business complains that many graduates are unprepared for entry-level jobs. By the 1990s one out of four black males in their twenties were either in jail or on probation for major crimes. Who will convince at-risk and direction-less youth that the minimum wage offered by McDonalds beats the hundreds of dollars per day gained by selling illegal, but widely used, drugs? Philosopher coaches are no panacea for the nation's ills, but as mentors for our youth they are a national treasure.

Their diversion and possible decline are all the more regrettable when we consider the special instructional circumstances of the coach-player relationship. It is a voluntary union—athletes seek coaches, and this pursuit makes a coach's environment of instruction especially effective. Kids listen to coaches. Similarly, as compared to classroom teachers, coaches enjoy special opportunities as role models and mentors. And surely one of the coaches' obligations, no matter what the stress and demands of the job, is to mentor young people.

One key mentoring objective is to forge in young people the strength of character to not compromise their integrity. Again, it's a matter of values. The pressures to forsake our values are endless; we fear failure and are all too often urged to go along with others, to please our boss, or break the rules for a competitive advantage. It takes strength of character to maintain integrity throughout one's career and life. Strong character is an ideal the philosopher coach is well positioned to teach. This means teaching integrity: the importance of telling the truth, fulfilling commitments, and living up to one's word. It means teaching values: the importance of not cheating, even when we are sure we won't get caught. To teach integrity means to teach the importance of taking responsibility for our actions and refusing to compromise our values, the importance of standing up for what we think is right, even when it may be unpopular.

Although no one prevails without some misdeeds and actions that fall short of pure integrity, a commitment to live and work with integrity is worthwhile for at least two profound reasons. First, integrity is a powerful professional asset, and its absence can be a burdensome liability. Although some unsavory characters on occasion may succeed, the odds are that their behavior will eventually catch up with them. In business, for example, people with a lack of integrity are usually found out. Most career paths are narrow, and a lack of integrity will nearly always surface through reference checking. Winston Churchill perhaps said it best in a 1941 speech:

> The only guide to a man is his conscience. The only shield to his memory is the rectitude and sincerity of his actions. It is very

imprudent to walk through life without this shield because we are so often mocked by the failure of our hopes and the upsetting of our calculations. But with this shield, however the fates may play, we march always in the ranks of honor.

Secondly, integrity is not only in one's professional self-interest, it is also essential to a satisfying life and to self-esteem. At some point late in life we all must ask with a critical eye: "Am I pleased with what I've done and proud of the *way* I've done it?" The famous words of Thomas Jefferson are worth remembering: "Whenever you are to do a thing, though it can never be known but to yourself, ask yourself how you would feel were all the world looking at you, and act accordingly."

Finally, there is the question of values as emphasized by all philosopher coaches. Americans, like all people, love heroes, and many of our most cherished heroes come from the world of sports. What are the qualities worthy of mass respect and emulation? Are they merely feats of triumph, superior physical capabilities, and talent? Should the dashing and dazzling be valued as heroes for their sports achievements alone? It is coaches who, by setting the quality and characteristics of teams and sporting competitions, often determine the correct answers. Failure by coaches to act as guardians of these values and to teach about them risks our losing them in future generations. It invites a weaker society.

The challenge is before us. Lombardi's total commitment to excellence, Hamilton's perspectives on life and athletics, Hayes's ten elements of leadership and concept of paying forward, Counsilman's hierarchy of human needs, Cerutty's Stotan creed, and Wooden's pyramid of success, all contain many virtues that modern coaches should strive to maintain and build upon. These are means of guiding youth, building character, instilling integrity, and pointing the way for youngsters to become confident self-reliant adults.

No challenge is greater, but the philosopher coach provides reminders to us all that it can be done, and the rewards—in the long-run—are ample indeed. That challenge is what makes the coaching profession more than a commercial enterprise. Meeting that challenge can make winners of us all. It takes us *Beyond Winning*.

Postscript

Dwight D. Eisenhower was an outstanding football player at Army. Gerald Ford played at Michigan, George Schultz at Princeton. Jack and Bobby Kennedy were devoted to athletics, and Nixon, Carter, Reagan, and Bush are all avid sports enthusiasts. Carter and Bush still work out regularly. Though these world leaders may not have had sufficient skills to compete as professional athletes, one fact is unmistakably clear: they did compete.

It's not mere coincidence that leaders, entrepreneurs, and managers at all levels share a common commitment to athletics. Participation in sports is uniformly a common denominator in their personal development and success. The lessons of competitive sports, including proper perspectives on winning and losing, prepare us for life's challenges. Competitive sport is a microcosm of daily life, and the physical and mental strains of athletic competition prepare us for the ups and downs of life.

One of the main arguments underlying *Beyond Winning* is that athletics, properly coached, provides a special arena of learning about oneself and about life. Athletic experiences are important to the process of human development and to the building of leadership skills. Participation in athletics bodes well for success and happiness, regardless of the quality level of performance or the monetary rewards. In short, sport for sport's sake is a top social value. The old saying "It's not whether you win or lose that counts but how you played the game" hungers for the sequel "and how you grow from the experience."

These arguments have testable propositions:

1. The proportion of leaders with significant backgrounds in athletics is higher than for the total population.

2. Given that men have had greater involvement in sports than women, both in intensity and years, men have been advantaged relative to women in the quest for leadership positions.

3. As women's involvement in sports, now rapidly expanding, continues to climb toward parity with men, the proportion of women in leadership positions will climb.

4. The proportion of women taking over new positions of leadership will have strong athletic backgrounds compared to the total population of women.

Although definitional and measurement problems abound in properly isolating the relevant variables and testing (to confirm or deny) these propositions, statisticians and other experts agree that measurement and hypothesis testing can be undertaken. *Beyond Winning* sets an agenda for more research, and it is hoped that scholars and educators will pursue these research lines to confirm or deny the propositions listed here and to discover new ones for our consideration.

References

Chapter 1

Cartwright, G. (1969, October 24). The unlikely Vincification of Sonny Jurgenson. *Life*, pp. 49-51.

A coach of champions: Advice to businessmen on how to lead. (1967, February 20). *U.S. News and World Report*, p. 14.

Flynn, G. (Ed.) (1973). *Vince Lombardi on football*. New York: New York Graphics Society.

Heinz, W.C. (1968, January 29). I miss the fire on Sunday. *Life*, pp. 121-122.

Johnson, W. (1969, March 3). ARARARARARAGH! *Sports Illustrated*, pp. 28-33.

Kramer, J. (1968). *Instant replay*. Evanston, IL: Holtzman Press.

Kramer, J. (1970, September 11). We played for Lombardi. *Life*, pp. 53-54.

Kramer, J. (1972). *Lombardi: Winning is the only thing*. New York: World Book.

Lombardi, V., & Cohane, T. (1961, October 24). The Packers pay the price. *Look*, pp. 103-111.

Maule, T. (1962, January 8). The day of devastation. *Sports Illustrated*, pp. 13-18.

Moritz, C. (1963). *A current biography*. New York: H.W. Wilson.

Smith, M. (1962, December 7). The miracle maker of Green Bay, Wisconsin. *Life*, pp. 49-52.

A special madness. (1970, September 14). *Newsweek*, p. 123.

Starr, B. (1967). *Quarterbacking.* Englewood Cliffs, NJ: Prentice/Hall.

A team for all time. (1970, September 11). *Life*, **69**, pp. 53-54.

Walsh, B., & Dickey, G. (1990). *Building a champion.* New York: St. Martin's Press.

Wind, H.W. (1962, December 8). The sporting scene: Packerland. *New Yorker*, pp. 213-230.

Underwood, J. (1969, July 28). We're going to win—You better believe it. *Sports Illustrated*, pp. 18-23.

Chapter 2

Berkow, I. (1982, May 2). Emerson's writings inspiring to Hayes. *New York Times*, p. C-7.

Brondfield, J. (1977, September). Explosive Woody Hayes. *Readers Digest*, pp. 98-102.

Hamelin, J. (1987, March 13). Was he a hero or an Ahab? *Sacramento Bee*, p. C-1.

Hayes, W.W. (1969). *Hot line to victory.* Columbus: Ohio State University.

Hornung, P. (1982, November 7). I don't live in the past . . . Woody Hayes. *Columbus Dispatch*, p. 9.

Leroux, C. (1982, June 10). Woody Hayes hero? It's Emerson, by a yard. *Chicago Tribune*, pp. 4-1, 4-6.

Ousted Hayes still heaps praise at OSU. (1979, January 21). *Columbus Dispatch*, p. D-2.

Strode, G. (1987, March 13). President honors Hayes as "legend." *Columbus Dispatch*, p. A-1.

Vare, R. (1974). *Buckeye.* New York: Harpers Magazine Press.

Chapter 3

Alcindor, L., & Olsen, J. (1969, November 10). A year of turmoil and decision. *Sports Illustrated*, p. 38.

Capouya, J. (1986, December). Zen and the art of baseball: In retirement, an old master looks back. *Sport Magazine*, p. 140.

Chapin, D., & Prugh, J. (1973). *The wizard of Westwood.* Boston: Houghton/Mifflin.

Harman, G.L. (1948, September). They ask me why I teach. *NEA Journal.*

Lessons from Japan's athletes. (1989, November 22). *Sacramento Bee*, p. G-2.

Starr, B. (1972). *A perspective on victory.* Chicago: Follett Press.

Tharp, R.G., & Gallimore, R. (1976, January). Basketball's John Wooden—What a coach can teach a teacher. *Psychology Today*, pp. 75-78.

Wolff, A. (1989, April 3). A coach and his champion. *Sports Illustrated*, pp. 94-111.

Wooden, J. (1966). The creed I live by. In L. King (Ed.), *Courage to conquer* (p. 29). Westwood, NJ: F.H. Revell.

Wooden, J. (1972). *They call me coach: As told to Jack Tobin.* Waco, TX: Word Books.

Wooden, J. (1984). *Pyramid of success* [Videotape]. Eugene, OR: Westcom Productions.

Wooden's winning way. (1972, January 14). *Los Angeles Times*.

Chapter 4

Cecil, B. (1978, April 27). Counsilman: Innovator, photographer, coach. *Indiana Daily Student.*

Counsilman, J.E. (1968). *The science of swimming.* Englewood Cliffs, NJ: Prentice/Hall.

Counsilman, J.E. (1977). *Competitive swimming manual for coaches and swimmers.* Bloomington, IN: Counsilman Co.

Counsilman, J.E. (1987, November 12). Coaches can be their own scientists. *American Coach*, p. 4.

Denny, D. (1968, April 2). Swimming is more than science to Counsilman. *Indianapolis News*, p. 25.

Hammel, B. (1990, February 4). 90 kids make Doc's exit excellent. *Sunday Herald Times* (Bloomington, IN).

Isaacson, M. (1990, February 4). The final bows: Doc and the shoe say so long. *Chicago Tribune*, pp. 3-1, 3-10.

Novak, C. (1990, June). "Doc" retires. *Our Indiana*, p. 7.

Silverstein, L. (1989, January 27). Hoosiers coach's accomplishments defy imagination. *Indiana Daily Student*, pp. 17, 20.

Sutton, S. (1990, March 4). IU made big splash with long time coach. *The Courier-Journal* (Bloomington, IN), pp. C-1, C-12.

Chapter 5

Baack, L. (Ed.) (1975). *The worlds of Brutus Hamilton.* Mountain View, CA: Tafnews Press.

Brutus Hamilton slated to be named coach of U.S. Olympic trackmen Saturday. (1952, January 31). *New York Herald Tribune*, p. 23.

Daley, A. (1952, February 1). Helsinki bound. *New York Times*, p. 28.

Grieve, C. (1952). Sports Parade. *San Francisco Examiner*, Sports section, p. 1.

Hamilton, B. (1954). A four-minute mile in '54? *Journal of the American Association for Health, Physical Education, & Recreation*, **25(5)**, 7-8, 43.

Levitt, E. (1965, June 13). Win for Brutus. *Tribune* (Oakland, CA), p. 51.

Russia big threat. (1952, February 5). *New York-Journal American*, p. 21.

Scott, J. (1965, June 22). Of Brutus's job on Proverb. *Berkeley Daily Gazette*, p. 5.

Chapter 6

Connery, D. (1958, November 10). The amazing Herb Elliott. *Sports Illustrated*, pp. 67-69.

Bannister, R. (1960, September 19). Ticking golden moments. *Sports Illustrated*, pp. 28, 33.

Boyle, R. (1960, March 28). Ron and Don by the sea. *Sports Illustrated*, pp. 22-27.

Elliott, H. (1960). *The Herb Elliott story*. New York: Thomas Nelson & Sons.

Maule, T. (1960, May 30). New Herb Elliott. *Sports Illustrated*, pp. 10-13.

Myers, L. (1977). *Training with Cerutty*. Mountain View, CA: World Publications.

Smith, L. (1960, August). Cranky genius of the track. *Coronet*, pp. 129-133.

Chapter 7

Callahan, T. (1989, October 9). The fall of the genius coach: Ten years are all a body can stand. *Newsweek*, p. 82.

Phillips, B. (1985, December). Basketball's legend revisited. *Scholastic Coach*, pp. 21, 42-47.

Wilbon, M. (1990, June 24). A reluctant paragon. *Sacramento Bee*, p. D-4.

Credits

Quotations in the Introduction from "A Coach of Champions: Advice to Businessmen on How to Lead," February 20, 1967, *U.S. News and World Report*, p. 14. Copyright 1967 by U.S. News and World Report. Reprinted by permission.

Chapter 1

Photos on pages 1, 5, and 9 courtesy of Chance Brockway.

Quotations from *Vince Lombardi on Football* by G. Flynn (Ed.), 1973, New York: New York Graphics Society. Copyright 1973 by Wallynn, Inc. Reprinted by permission.

Quotations from the following article are reprinted courtesy of *Sports Illustrated* from the March 3, 1969 issue. Copyright © 1969, Time, Inc. "ARARARARARAGH!" by W. Johnson. All rights reserved.

Quotations from *Instant Replay* by J. Kramer, 1968, Evanston, IL: Holtzman Press. Copyright 1968 by Jerry Kramer and Dick Schaap. Reprinted and adapted by permission.

Quotations and Vince Lombardi's Head Coaching Record from *Lombardi: Winning Is the Only Thing* by J. Kramer, 1972, New York: World Book. Copyright 1972 by Jerry Kramer and Maddick Manuscripts, Inc. Reprinted by permission.

Quotations from the phone conversation with Jerry Kramer (March 20, 1991) used with permission.

Quotations from the following article are reprinted courtesy of *Sports Illustrated* from the January 8, 1962 issue. Copyright © 1962, Time, Inc. "The Day of Devastation" by T. Maule. All rights reserved.

Quotations from the following article are reprinted courtesy of *Sports Illustrated* from the January 27, 1986 issue. Copyright © 1986, Time, Inc. "A Team for All Time." All rights reserved.

Quotations from the following article are reprinted courtesy of *Sports Illustrated* from the July 28, 1969 issue. Copyright © 1969, Time, Inc. "We're Going to Win—You Better Believe It" by J. Underwood. All rights reserved.

Chapter 2

Photos on pages 19, 28, and 35 courtesy of Chance Brockway.

Quotations from "Emerson's Writings Inspiring to Hayes" by I. Berkow, May 2, 1982, *New York Times*, p. C-7. Copyright © 1982 by The New York Times Company. Reprinted by permission.

Quotations from the phone conversation with Archie Griffin (February 13, 1991) used with permission.

Quotations and Table 2.1 from *Hot Line to Victory* by W.W. Hayes, 1969, Columbus: Ohio State University. Copyright 1969 by W.W. Hayes. Reprinted and adapted by permission.

Woody Hayes's Head Coaching Record courtesy of the Ohio State University Sports Information Office.

Chapter 3

Photos on pages 43, 51, and 67, John Wooden's Honors, and John Wooden's Head Coaching Record courtesy of the University of California, Los Angeles, Sports Information Office.

Quotations from the following article are reprinted courtesy of *Sports Illustrated* from the November 10, 1969 issue. Copyright © 1969, Time, Inc. "A Year of Turmoil and Decision" by L. Alcindor with J. Olsen. All rights reserved.

Quotations from *The Wizard of Westwood* by Dwight Chapin and Jethro Prugh. Copyright © 1983 by Dwight Chapin and Jethro Prugh. Reprinted by permission of Houghton Mifflin Company.

Poem on page 69 from "They Ask Me Why I Teach" by G.L. Harman, September 1948, *NEA Journal*. Copyright 1948 by the NEA. Reprinted by permission.

Quotations and Table 3.1 from "Basketball's John Wooden— What a Coach Can Teach a Teacher" by R.G. Tharp and R. Gallimore, January 1976, *Psychology Today*, pp. 75-78. Reprinted with permission from Psychology Today Magazine. Copyright © 1976 (Sussex Publishers, Inc.).

Quotations from the following article are reprinted courtesy of *Sports Illustrated* from the April 3, 1989 issue. Copyright © 1989, Time, Inc. "A Coach and His Champion" by A. Wolff. All rights reserved.

Quotations from "The Creed I Live By" by J. Wooden, 1966, in *Courage to Conquer* edited by LeRoy King, copyright 1967 by Fleming H. Revell Co. Used by permission of Fleming H. Revell Co.

Quotations from *They Call Me Coach: As Told to Jack Tobin* by J. Wooden, 1972, Waco, TX: Word Books. Copyright 1972 by Word, Incorporated. Reprinted by permission.

Quotations from *Pyramid of Success* [Videotape] by J. Wooden, 1984, Eugene, OR: Westcom Productions. Copyright 1984 by John Wooden and Westcom Productions. Reprinted by permission.

Figure 1 on page 48, John Wooden's Pyramid of Success, courtesy of John Wooden.

Quotations from the meeting with John Wooden (1987) used with permission.

Chapter 4

Photos on pages 75, 77, 81, 83, and Doc Counsilman's Head Coaching Record courtesy of the Indiana University Department of Intercollegiate Athletics.

Quotations from the conversation with Peter Andersen (September 30, 1990) used with permission.

Quotations from James E. Counsilman, *The Science of Swimming*, © 1968, pp. viii, ix, 342. Reprinted by permission of Prentice Hall, Englewood Cliffs, NJ.

Quotations from *Competitive Swimming Manual for Coaches and Swimmers* by J.E. Cousilman, 1977, Bloomington, IN: Counsilman Co. Copyright 1977 by Counsilman Co., Inc. Reprinted by permission.

Quotations from the conversation with Charles B. Hickcox (1990) used with permission.

Quotations from "IU Made Big Splash With Long Time Coach" by S. Sutton, March 4, 1990, *The Courier-Journal* (Bloomington, IN), pp. C-1, C-12. Copyright © 1990 by The Courier-Journal. Reprinted with permission.

Chapter 5

Photos on pages 99, 110, and 113 courtesy of Ed Kirwan Graphic Arts.

Quotations from *The Worlds of Brutus Hamilton* by L. Baack (Ed.), 1975, Mountain View, CA: Tafnews Press. Copyright 1975, Tafnews Press, Book Division of Track and Field News. Reprinted by permission.

Quotations from "A Four-Minute Mile in '54?" by B. Hamilton are reprinted with permission from the *Journal of Physical Education, Recreation & Dance*, **25**(5), pp. 7-8, 43. The *Journal* is a publication of the American Alliance for Health, Physical Education, Recreation and Dance, 1900 Association Drive, Reston, VA 22091.

Quotations from "Win for Brutus" by E. Levitt, June 13, 1965, *Sunday Tribune Sports* (Oakland, CA), p. 51. Copyright 1965 by Oakland Tribune. Reprinted by permission.

Quotations from the Brutus Hamilton archives and Brutus Hamilton's Head Coaching Facts used with the permission of Jean Runyon.

Quotations by Lon Spurrier used with permission.

Chapter 6

Photos on pages 129 and 152 courtesy of David H. Clarke.

Quotations from the following article are reprinted courtesy of *Sports Illustrated* from the November 10, 1958 issue. Copyright © 1960, Time, Inc. "The Amazing Herb Elliot" by D. Connery. All rights reserved.

Quotations from the following article are reprinted courtesy of *Sports Illustrated* from the September 19, 1960 issue. Copyright © 1960, Time, Inc. "Ticking Golden Moments" by R. Bannister. All rights reserved.

Acknowledgments

I am often asked what prompted me to write *Beyond Winning*. There are long and short answers to most questions, and reading *Beyond Winning* supplies the long answer. The short of it, however, is that the day after Woody Hayes died (March 15, 1987) I read an article in the sports section of the *Sacramento Bee* that upset me. Hayes was accused of often confusing football with war. I was angry with sportswriter Joe Hamelin, whom I thought confused ignorance with temperament. I wrote and told him so, and Mr. Hamelin deserves credit for getting me started.

A few months later, a dear old friend and renowned scholar, Donald McCloskey, Professor of Economics and History at the University of Iowa, came to the University of California, Davis to give a lecture. I told him about my ideas for the book, and he was extremely enthusiastic. Several months later he published a paper entitled "The Limits of Expertise: If You're So Smart Why Ain't You Rich?" in *The American Scholar* (Summer, 1988) in which he cited *Beyond Winning* as soon forthcoming. Don deserves major credit for making me stick to it.

Many others provided specialized advice and assistance on the coaches selected. Jim Sochor, our athletic director at Davis, met with me at an early stage to discuss the purpose of the book and the chapters on Lombardi and Hayes. Jerry Kramer, the noted author and authority on Lombardi, shared stories on Lombardi and provided some hard-to-find facts. Al Stavitsky, Marvin Homan,

John Mount, and Bob Epskamp helped me locate materials on Hayes and advised me on the chapter on him.

Students at the Sports Information Office at UCLA provided me with printed matter on Coach Wooden, and I am grateful to John Wooden for inviting me to his home and for taking a personal interest in the project. My colleague Doug Minnis first brought to my attention the *Psychology Today* (January 1976, pp. 75-78) article on Wooden entitled, "What a Coach Can Teach a Teacher" by R.G. Tharp and R. Gallimore.

Doc and Marge Counsilman kindly invited me to their home, and to a retirement dinner for Doc where I met nearly all of his great swimmers. Pete Andersen, Charlie Hickcox, and Marge were especially helpful to me in revising the chapter on Counsilman.

Jean Runyon has been instrumental in providing me with materials on her father Brutus Hamilton. Her personal encouragement has been a constant source of inspiration to me; and several of Brutus's great athletes, Dave Maggard, Lon Spurrier, Don Bowden, and George Linn have given me timely help on the chapter on Hamilton.

George Linn, my college roommate, who stayed at Portsea with Percy Cerutty in 1960, provided me with invaluable information on Cerutty. Don Bowden, Doc Counsilman, and Lon Spurrier also added their reflections on personally meeting Percy and on being at the Portsea Training Camp.

Jerry Hume and Jim Meyer played a key role advising me on the revision of Chapter 7, and I am especially grateful for their suggestions to improve it.

Many friends, relatives, and colleagues have read portions or all of the book. Their collective encouragement and advice assured the completion of the first draft. They are: Joe Naughten, C.B. Sung, Joe Vigil, Bob Ebel, Rob Anex, Rob Andersen, Ted Goyette, Doug Nikias, Dana Wilson, Mike Goralka, Paul Cummings, Ann Marie Georgi, Bob Brown, Dan Walters, John Wells, Bert Swanston, Mike Hurlston, Stephan Passalaqua, Surrey Walton, Rhodes Walton, Linda Walton, Joe Giovanazzi, Archie Griffin, Richard Easterlin, John Bunting, Larry Swanston, Wally Hawley, Marcia Smith, John Hardie, Max and Lorraine Walton, Sam Bell, Doug Ramsey, Thomas Horton, Bruce Maxwell, George Hume, Jack Hume, John Claerhout, Clark Kerr, Mike and Ev Roberts, Sue Walker, Smokey Murphy, William Pritchard, Jim Burden, Peter Bush, Don and Dee Schilling, Cheryl Turner, Mark Arnold, Curt Robinson, Joel Skornika, Jan Seahorn, Myron Sugarman, and Jim Kaspari.

Charlie Gomez, Steve Gerhart, and Phil Graves proofread the full first draft and helped me improve the organization and style. Phil deserves credit for suggesting the subtitle, but I claim credit for the title. Steve assisted in obtaining the permissions on the many quotes and finding the pictures we have used. His help has been critical throughout the final stages of completion.

Valuable clerical assistance was provided by Jenie Silva, and Josephine Chu patiently translated my longhand scrawl into typed verse. Opritsa Popa met request after request by me for help in the library to find research materials.

Lastly, the works of earlier writers on the coaches and issues discussed in *Beyond Winning* are forthrightly acknowledged. These earlier works were essential to the study.

About the Author

Dividing time between athletics and academics is nothing new to Gary Walton—he's been doing it since he was a freshman at the University of California at Berkeley. At that time, he was influenced by the legendary track coach Brutus Hamilton, whose philosophy emphasized athletics as part of personal development.

Dr. Walton continues to live by this philosophy at the University of California at Davis where he is professor and coach. In addition to being the founding dean of the university's School of Management, he is president of The Foundation for Teaching Economics, a professor of economics and management, and an assistant coach for the university's track team. Dr. Walton received his doctorate in economics from the University of Washington and has authored and coauthored eight books in economics and American economic history.

Dr. Walton's duties on the track include coaching middle-distance and distance runners. He is also a devoted runner himself. As for his coaching philosophy, Dr. Walton emphasizes dedication and hard work, preferring that runners achieve their personal best rather than worry about getting their names in the record books.